Raymond

TUNNEL VISION

AUSTIN MACAULEY PUBLISHERS™
LONDON • CAMBRIDGE • NEW YORK • SHARJAH

Copyright © Raymond Gartland (2020)

The right of Raymond Gartland to be identified as author of this work has been asserted by the author in accordance with section 77 and 78 of the Copyright, Designs and Patents Act 1988.

All rights reserved. No part of this publication may be reproduced, stored in a retrieval system, or transmitted in any form or by any means, electronic, mechanical, photocopying, recording, or otherwise, without the prior permission of the publishers.

Any person who commits any unauthorised act in relation to this publication may be liable to criminal prosecution and civil claims for damages.

This is a work of fiction. Names, characters, businesses, places, events, locales, and incidents are either the products of the author's imagination or used in a fictitious manner. Any resemblance to actual persons, living or dead, or actual events is purely coincidental.

A CIP catalogue record for this title is available from the British Library.

ISBN 9781528913768 (Paperback)
ISBN 9781528992442 (Hardback)
ISBN 9781528929875 (ePub e-book)
ISBN 9781398418219 (Audiobook)

www.austinmacauley.com

First Published (2020)
Austin Macauley Publishers Ltd
25 Canada Square
Canary Wharf
London
E14 5LQ

Acknowledgements

Mr Michael Newnan—Kildare, Ireland

Michael Dawnay—Wicklow, Ireland

William O Connor—Waterford, Ireland

Ronald Mc Cann—Dublin, Ireland

John O Connell—Dublin, Ireland

Prologue

This story was inspired by true events.

The three main characters in this book are real people. Only one character has asked to change his name for legal reasons. The locations in this book have been changed to prevent legal actions on conspiracy charges.

For this reason, I have disguised all locations and currencies. The three main characters are intelligent, clever members of the underworld. This bank robbery would have been the biggest in history. It is every bank robber's dream to find one like this. One character in this book has multiple convictions for bank robberies.

This job would have been carried out exactly the way it is described in this book, but due to unforeseen circumstances, the job could not go ahead. Names of places in this book are fictitious, and if this book describes an actual place, that is a coincidence. When you read this book, you should get the feeling that this job could have taken place in your town or anywhere in any country around the world. The writer wants every reader to fantasise that they are a character in this book. If anybody is offended by anything said or language used in this book, the writer apologises unreservedly.

Chapter 1

It was March 2000 and Charlie was having a drink in McCarthy's Pub, waiting for Billy and Mick to come from the city to join him for a social drink.

Charlie was not from Charlestown; he was born overseas. While waiting for his two loyal comrades, he popped out to the local shop to get the newspaper. He returned and sat waiting for his friends. When they arrive, they will discuss where they could do their next big job; all of them had bad luck experiences of doing time for jobs that went wrong in some way or another.

Charlie opened the newspaper. On the inside page was a photograph of the local bank with the headlines saying: *"Bank must retain the old façade walls when building the new bank because the old walls were over a hundred and fifty years old."* It was a heritage site. It was only a hundred yards from where Charlie was sitting, having a beer waiting for his friends.

Mick was just driving into town with Billy – also known to his mates as *Billy the kid*. It was only a social night out but Charlie had invited them down to discuss the next big heist he had in mind. Charlie never liked doing armed bank jobs, but Billy the kid had a passion for them. Michael was a man that was very cold and calm to strangers. He trusted nobody, and he choose very reluctantly who he worked with. With him you're in or you're out but no in-between.

'What does Charlie have in mind for us, do you think?' asked Billy.

'I don't know if he has anything,' Mick said. 'But if he has, you can be sure it will be a good one; he always comes up with the best plans. Well, he was noted for his personal bravery and excellent organisation during the past 15 years.'

'Anyways, we are meeting him in McCarthy's at 7 pm,' said Billy.

'And he is there right now,' said Mick, 'of course he is. Charlie doesn't wait around for nobody; if he says seven, take my word, Billy, at five minutes past seven, Charlie will leave even if it's only a social meeting.'

'What time is it now, Mick?'

'Ten to seven, and how far more is it?' said Billy.

'Six miles,' said Mick. 'He said be there at seven and not to phone and say you're on the way. He will only say you're going to be fucking late. And he would fuck off right now.'

'Okay,' said Billy as Mick drove into Johnson Street and parked down the road from McCarthy's Pub. 'Come on,' said Billy jumping out of the car.

'We have only a few minutes left. When we walk into the pub you will see Charlie look at his watch. If we are late by a minute he will say, "why are ye late?" but if we are early by a few minutes he will say "nice one boys, you are on time",' Mick said.

As Mick and Billy walked into the pub, there was Charlie looking at his watch and said, 'Nice one boys, you two are on time. I love to see men keep the time no matter what or where they have to go. What are you both drinking?'

'The usual whiskey for me,' said Mick, 'and you, Billy?'

'Just spring water for me, Charlie, I will be driving back tonight.'

'No, Billy, nobody is driving anywhere tonight. Your beds are all made up at my house so we can have a good drink and chat, and there's a late club upstairs for whatever ye are into. The women are on tap upstairs, and we can drink where we like up there with nobody listening to us. So, what are you drinking, Billy,' said Charlie again. 'And this time I want an answer.'

'Well, in that case make it a large one. Would ye look at that blonde model over there that I would only die for,' Billy said. 'Charlie, will you ask her to pee in a champagne glass and put two ice cubes in it, and I will sink it down the hatch.'

'For that, Billy, you're on large beers tonight,' Charlie said. They all laughed, and the model knew they were making a joke of her.

'Well, Billy, cross her off your list for tonight,' said Charlie.

'She didn't hear or see anything,' said Mick. 'She doesn't have to hear you. I will tell her in a minute what you said when I buy her another drink!'

'Yes,' said Charlie. 'I bought her one before ye came in. So do you think you are getting what I paid for?'

'No way, boys, she is mine. You're always one step ahead, Charlie.'

'I would never boldly go where Charlie has gone before,' Mick said with Billy hysterically laughing out loud.

'Listen,' said Charlie, 'you two are new in town tonight and upstairs are a lot of hungry floozy girls.' Charlie called the barman, drink for the boys and the same for Marilyn over there.

'Back in a minute, lads. Must suss out this blonde Marilyn for later. And then when I come back, we can get down to talking business,' Charlie said as he walked to the table where the blonde model was sitting.

'Marilyn, you look so alone there.'

'I am waiting for my date to turn up,' she replied as Charlie sat beside her, hoping the boys did not hear her say that, and he would only look like a fool if they did.

'That's my friends over there Mick and Billy, down for the night for a drinking session. But I don't understand how their beautiful wives put up with them never at home,' Charlie said with a smirk on his face hoping that she was not a married man lover.

'Marilyn, I will go back to the boys and give your date a fighting chance but we might bump into you upstairs later on.' As Charlie left the table Marilyn said, 'My name is Jane, not Marilyn.'

'My name is Charlie and you are the best-looking Marilyn Monroe I've ever seen in my life.' Marilyn smiled.

At the bar Mick said, 'What did she say to you, Charlie?'

'Well, if you really want to know, she said tell the two married men with you I saw them laughing at me.'

'We are not married,' both Mick and Billy said at the same time.

'I told her none of us were married,' said Charlie with a smirk on his face.

'Okay,' said Mick, 'so we all have a chance with her later in the nightclub.'

'Yes,' said Charlie with a grin on his face again. The boys looked at Charlie, knowing he did them no favours for that few minutes he spoke to Marilyn. 'She has a date any way, boys, so we can all kiss her ass goodbye tonight. Any way we must find a corner to sit and chat about something really good I have in my mind. Come on down the back, and we find a spot.'

The pub was starting to fill up. Friday night is always a busy night in McCarthy's. A thousand people can fit in this super pub; it is the biggest pub in town. They found a quiet corner to chat. Charlie took out the paper he bought in the shop before the boys arrived. 'Lads, I had nothing in mind for us tonight. But while I was waiting for you to call, I saw this photograph of the bank around the corner. Look at what it says: *"Bank must retain all the old wall structure while they are building the new bank".* So they are building a new bank around the corner. And retaining the old walls but look at the writing underneath. It's going to be a holding centre for the region. Do you know what that is about?' asked Charlie.

'Yes,' said Billy, 'they are going to build a new bank with the old front walls retained.'

'Yes,' said Charlie. 'Billy, new banks are harder to rob than old banks.'

'Yes, they are,' said Charlie and Mick waiting for more to be said. As Charlie looked at his watch he said, 'When I sort out this idea in my head, I will let ye know more.

'Would that be tonight?' said Mick impatiently. 'Well, put it this way, I think right now we could rob that bank. Holding centre banks holds money for all the other banks in the region. That means they will have many millions in the vault of that bank.'

'I believe that,' says Mick as Billy eyes lit up. 'But it will be a brand-new vault,' Mick continued. 'Three-foot hard reinforced concrete, the hardest cement mix in the world,' Billy said laughing. 'A dentist could not drill a hole in that vault. Time locks. Delay systems. Sensors. All the new security that you can think will be there in that bank.'

Charlie said, 'I told you boys I have an idea in my head called, *"Tunnel Vision",* so leave it to me for a week and you come down again and I will have a plan put together. So now, let's enjoy ourselves for the night, and get some ladies to take home.'

'How can I put my mind on floozies when I am counting millions, and where am I going to hide it?' said Mick.

'Counting millions and thinking of floozies are my two favourite pastimes,' said Billy.

'Mine too,' said Charlie.

'But it's ladies now so let's head up to the other end of the bar. It's your round, Mick, don't be shy, and you also have to get a drink from Marilyn,' laughing out loud, 'and her date. You have to give him a drink as well,' Mick said.

Billy was laughing on the way towards where Marilyn was sitting.

'Look,' said Mick, 'she has a sugar daddy, fucking gold digger she is.'

'Well, in that case,' said Charlie, 'only I can afford her.'

'If we all get an equal share on this one, we can all afford her,' said Billy.

'Will it be three ways this time,' Billy continued, 'or does the boss get more?'

'You get paid for what you put into it, Billy,' said Charlie. 'I do a lot of work behind the scene which takes up a lot of my time while ye are enjoying yourselves. So if I put a lot more work in, am I not entitled to get more out?'

'That's true,' said Mick. 'You have to do all the work and sort all the problems, and make sure everything goes right so we do agree, you should get a bigger share.'

'Right, boys, no more shop talk in the pub tonight. How can I put this plan together if you keep interrupting me?'

'So you're still planning it while we're drinking?' said Mick. 'And I thought we were chasing some women.'

'I can do the planning and the chasing at the same time because I cannot switch off the brain from the plan. I am planning the Tunnel, we have to dig from the derelict house across the road so I am planning to get the bank in my head but I'm also planning to get Marilyn in my bed tonight.'

'Which one comes first?' said Billy with a laugh.

'I will,' said Charlie, 'because she is so good looking,' with a bigger laugh.

'I am talking about the bank,' said Billy with a knot in his stomach from holding in a loud laugh.

'I would too,' said Mick, 'if I get Marilyn tonight.'

'But she said she doesn't like married men,' said Charlie laughing.

'I know what you're laughing at, Charlie, you bollocks,' said Billy.

'What is that?' said Charlie with another grin.

Billy's answer to Mick was, 'I bet that bollocks told Marilyn that we were fucking married.'

'You're right,' said Mick, 'the bollocks did tell her that we were married. He can't keep a straight face.'

'Well,' said Billy, 'when Marilyn's sugar daddy boyfriend goes to that toilet, I will push him out the back door pretending I am security, and he must leave.'

'Leave the poor bastard alone,' said Charlie. 'That old pensioner should be off the premises by 9 pm.'

'And he still here and it's nearly 10 pm,' said Mick, 'and if Charlie's girlfriend, Celine, pulls up outside in the silver jeep, Charlie must hide. Speak of the devil, boys, here is my girlfriend in the back door, and she's walking towards us with a serious face.'

'Boys,' said Charlie, 'forgot to tell you if my bird turns up in the pub, she will not let ye bring floozies home to our house. She's a very strict Jewish girl.'

Chapter 2

Next morning the two boys were driving back to the city.

'My head is wrecked from that drink last night. Billy, slow down the fucking car, that cop car just clocked you speeding, and here he comes after you.'

'Fuck it,' said Billy. 'Hope you have all your documents for the car.'

'Pull in, Billy, the siren and lights are on.'

'Mick, get out my documents from the glove box.'

The cop came to the window. 'Good morning, Sergeant,' said Billy.

'You were speeding, sir.'

'Sorry, Sergeant.'

'Doing 40 in a 30. I must write you a ticket.'

'Okay, sir.'

'What is your full name, sir?'

'William Joseph O'Connor.'

'So you are the bold B.T.K. Billy the Kid.'

'That is what they call me.'

'Your cowboy friend looks like one of the long riders. So who would you be, cowboy?'

'My name is Michael Dawnay, Sergeant.'

'Dawnay – is a French name, cowboy?'

'That is where my granddaddy came from, Sergeant. No such thing as a French cowboy, sir. No, Sergeant, just hard-working, honest farmers, Sergeant.'

'Well, its bank holiday Monday so I will let you go with just the ticket. Go and take it easy, kid.'

Billy drove off slowly.

'Listen to the cop, and take it easy, Billy, because if I get sick it will be on you; I will do it,' said Mick.

'What happened with Charlie and Celine last night?'

'Charlie was telling her how much he loved her.'

'Who? Celine?'

'No, stupid, he was telling Marilyn he loved her over Celine's shoulder and Celine caught him and kneed him in the balls with a smile of innocence.'

'Ha,' said Mick, 'served him right.'

'The fucker Charlie had Marilyn wait all for himself,' said Billy.

'When we decided not to go near Marilyn and she was on her own, Charlie could not leave Celine with us to make a sly move on Marilyn because he could not trust us foxes with minding the henhouse,' said Mick. 'The floozy girl you got in the club was nicer than mine. Charlie was going mad when we brought two birds home and Celine did not mind us at all.'

'Ha ha,' said Mick, 'the fucker wanted us to do the Pope on our own because Celine showed up.'

'What do you think of the Tunnel job he is onto?' said Mick.

'Well, with me, Mick, it's in and out is always the best way, grab what you can carry, no real planning, hustle. I used to do one every week,' said Billy.

'Every week?' said Mick.

'You fucker, you did two a week some weeks, that's if I needed a week off to go on holidays,' said Billy.

'Well, Billy, they don't call you Billy the Kid or BTK for no reason. You must have robbed every bank in the county.'

'Some of them twice,' said Billy.

'But you know, Charlie won't allow this unless he approves it. A few days and the boys are back in town again.'

Charlie's phone rang. It was his Celine's father on the other end. He sounded very upset. 'Hello, Charlie, it's Joseph here.'

'Hello, Joseph,' said Charlie.

'Can you help me?' said Joseph.

'I will try. You know I am building a house costing a few million.'

'I do. Celine told me about it. Do you know O'Brien the builders?' asked Joseph.

'I do.'

'Well, Charlie, he is after robbing me out of a lot of money. Is there anything you could do for me? They are short cutting the build and charging me exorbitant prices.'

'I know them, Joseph,' said Charlie, 'they rob everybody. How did he get the job to build a new bank? They will rob the bank as well.'

'You know rightly, Charlie,' said Joseph. 'They will take that bank to the cleaners for every cent they can get.'

'The bank can well afford it, Charlie, they have millions. I can't afford them, O'Brien's robbing me.'

'I will call and have a look at the work O'Brien builders did on your new house, and I will then tell you what to do about it. I will see you tomorrow, Joseph, and will have a look at the house,' Charlie hung up the phone and said to the boys, 'The same fucking builder, O'Brien, is building the bank and my father-in-law's house. He is robbing my fiancée's poor father out of a lot of money. I will fix O'Brien for doing that to him.'

'We will sort him out,' said Billy.

'No, Billy,' said Charlie, 'I have a better idea for him.'

The phone rang in the bank manager's office: 'Mr Regan from the town hall said the planning permission was passed last night at the town hall meeting.'

'That's good. We will transfer all the business next week to the other office in Dominic Street, counsellor,' said the bank manager.

'So we get to work on the rebuild right away.'

'It will be in the paper next week that we will have a brand new modern state-of-the-art central bank for our region next year.'

'Thank you, Mr Regan, and thank all the councillors for quickly sorting out our planning permission.'

The manager phoned O'Brien the builders to tell him the good news.

'I will get the work down to you this afternoon to guide you through the clear out of the whole building.'

'Okay, Mr O'Brien. The quicker we get started the quicker we will be back in our new bank.'

By the time Friday came, and the boys were down again Charlie had got the paper early this morning to see another write-up on the bank. Planning permission was passed on the new bank build on the front page in big bold writing.

'Planning,' said Charlie to himself, 'why didn't I think of the plans in the town hall planning office?'

Chapter 3

Friday night, 7 pm. Billy and Mick walked into McCarthy's pub. Charlie was sitting in the same spot reading the local paper. 'Well, boys,' said Charlie, 'did ye have a nice drive down?'

'There was a lot of traffic on the highways today,' said Billy.

'Did you have enough time to put a plan together for this new bank job, Charlie?' said Billy.

'I did, boys. I have the plan, and a very busy week running around.'

'By the way, we are working tonight,' said Charlie as he drank the last of his spring water. 'So let's go and get started.'

'Are we robbing the bank tonight?' said Mick.

'Are you fucking mad, Mick? The fucking bank is empty since today.'

'They are pulling it down next week, only the four main walls will be left. So what are we doing tonight, Charlie?' said Mick.

'Tell you in the car, come on it's getting dark.' In the car Charlie said, 'We are getting into the town hall planning office to get a set of plans of the bank. They had to lodge a set for the planning permission.'

On the way to the planning office Charlie spoke more. 'It's like this,' said Charlie, 'we will rob the plans of the rebuild of the bank, and we can use a nice scope from the hotel room every few weeks to see the progress of the build.'

'Yes,' said Billy.

'But tell us more of this plan, Charlie,' said Mick. They walked down the laneway into the back of the town hall. 'Not even a burglar alarm to be seen on the wall of the town hall,' said Charlie. 'And the town hall is closed down for the weekend. Mick, you keep an eye on the lane when me and Billy go in and get the plans and use your mobile phone to call us if anyone comes around.'

At the back of the town hall Charlie and Billy used their burgling skills to gain entry to the building. They opened the back door with some special skeleton keys Charlie had, so nobody would know they were in. So if there was no break in nothing would be missed. Charlie said to Billy, 'If you see or find money in here do not take it because they will know someone broke in.'

'Whatever you say, Charlie,' said Billy with a sulk on his face.

'All in good time, Billy, and you will have more money than you will ever spend in your lifetime. Trust my judgement,' said Charlie.

Chapter 4

The lock on the office door opened. Charlie said, 'This special lock pick set never lets me down.'

Charlie had on a miner's lamp on his head; Billy carried pocket light. 'I know where they keep the files,' Charlie said, 'because I was in here getting planning permission myself.'

And Billy jokingly said, 'There is nothing hard about finding the planning office, because all you have to do is follow the signs, and it's wrote on the door as well.'

Billy said, 'Charlie, how do you master the skills to opening them locks, they are five lever mortise Chubb locks, not easy to open.'

Charlie replied with a smirk on his face, 'They're no problem, if I am with you.'

'How about safes, Charlie? Can you open them because there is one over there in the corner?'

'Let me tell you again, Billy. We didn't come here for money, we came here for a set of plans.'

'Okay, Charlie, only asking.' In the planning room Charlie was searching the drawers for planning applications. There were walls of filing cabinets with "Planning" on them.

Charlie said to Billy, 'We find the drawer that says "Planning Approval".'

Upon searching Billy called Charlie and said, 'I found a cabinet saying "New Applications Approved".'

'Where is it?' asked Charlie.

'The one at the end of that side.' Charlie opened the drawer and rummaged through the bundles of planning applications and found the bank application in a big brown envelope. He put the envelope on the table and removed all the documents. He quickly searched, and he found an area map that was included with the planning application. He opened up the map and with his head light focused on a spot; Charlie took out a safety pin and focused on the part of the map and put a hole in it. Then he turned to Billy and said, 'Look around for a Xerox machine to copy this map.'

Billy came back from the other side of the room which was pitch dark and said there is one over there. Charlie went to the machine and photocopied the map, section by section, as it was too big for the Xerox to do in one print. He quickly returned to the table and put the map and all the application back into the envelope and placed it in the drawer where it was.

Billy said to Charlie, 'What are you doing? Why did you put pin hole in the map and put it back in the drawer?'

'All in good time, Billy. The day will come Billy when you will know why I did that, for now we leave it at that.'

Billy and Charlie quickly left the planning office. Charlie knelt down and picked the lock close. 'Right, we are out of here,' said Charlie. They left the building by the back door. Charlie knelt down again and picked the lock closed. They both climbed over the back wall into the laneway where Mick was waiting.

'Did you get what you wanted, Charlie?' said Mick.

'I did, I got what I wanted.'

'You were only in there ten minutes?'

'I know that. It doesn't take long to look into a few drawers and get a piece of paper.

'And I'm here waiting thinking that you would be in there all night.'

'I don't hang around them places; to me it's in and out.'

They walked to the end of the laneway and onto the street, Charlie with the plans up his sweatshirt. 'Will the bank take long to rob?' said Mick laughing at Charlie and Billy's success.

'About fifteen minutes,' said Charlie.

'Are you fucking serious – fifteen minutes?'

'Yes, Billy, but that will be at the last visit.'

'But it will take two hours to carry out the fucking money, Billy.'

Mick asked with a serious look of fear in his eyes from the streetlights, 'How much money is in the vault?'

At the car, Charlie said, 'From now on, we never talk about this bank job in the car or in any other building of any kind as every fucking place is getting bugged these days. So I will tell you this only once,' continued Charlie, 'and never bring it up again. Refer to money as bags of spuds if you have to ask.'

'How much?' Billy said, 'How much are we talking about?'

Billy waited to be shocked with the answer. Charlie answered him, cool and calm, 'Two hundred to three hundred million.'

Billy and Mick said "fuck" together.

'200 million bags of spuds,' said Billy and Mick at the same time laughing. 'We better sit down and talk about this.'

'I know we have a lot of talking to do about this, but we must be very careful where we talk,' said Charlie.

'I hope none of us talk in our sleep,' said Mick.

'Well,' Billy said, 'my bird would think I was dreaming of another bird.'

'What do you mean?' said Charlie.

'Well,' said Billy. 'If I dreamt of a room with two hundred million on the floor and I on top of it. It would be like having the best sex of my life.'

'A wet dream, so,' Mick said.

'That's right, Mick,' said Billy.

'She would think I was dreaming of a beautiful woman,' said Billy.

'That is normal,' said Charlie. 'I did it before. Adding best fucking shag you can imagine is having sex in a room full of money.'

Billy started laughing saying, 'I'm getting an erection talking about it.'

'You are not the only one getting hard on myself,' said Mick.

'Remember one thing, boys. In life there is no love more sincere then the love a man has for money.'

'I will rephrase that,' said Mick. 'There is no love more sincere than our girlfriends' love for our money.'

'A man might fall in love with a woman,' said Charlie, 'but a man is always in love with money.'

'Let's get home and look at the plans,' said Mick as the three jumped into the car. 'Now that we are finished early, can we go to the pub. We might run into Marilyn again?'

'I knew you would say that, Billy. Floozy women on your mind again.'

'Well, Charlie, if you did not use the word spuds for you know what.'

'For the record we don't know what you're talking about, Billy.'

'Look boys, I knew it would only take us ten minutes to get what I have.'

'The map,' said Mick. Charlie and Billy looked at Mick as he called himself an idiot for talking in the car.

'Anyway, Mick, you and Billy put Marilyn out of your head.'

'Why?' said Billy. 'Is she married to the sugar daddy?'

'No,' said Charlie.

'So what is it?' said Mick.

'Well, my friends,' Charlie said with a smile on his face. 'I pulled her the other night and had a wild night of sex with Marilyn. So get your own birds, she is mine now.'

'Who would boldly go where Charlie has gone before?' said Billy.

'Well, Charlie, did you wear rubber?'

'Why, Mick? She is clean girl,' said Charlie.

'Thanks, Charlie, for answering two questions at the same time. You didn't wear rubber, and now she's not clean any more, she is now off our lists,' said Billy.

'Fucking right,' said Mick. 'The whole jail knew Charlie had to get the warts burned off when he came in.'

'That's right,' said Billy. 'I heard him cry in the surgery when the doctors were burning the warts off with liquid nitrogen.'

'The walls are sound proof,' said Charlie.

'The sound proof only works one way; it leaves no sound in it, only leaves it out,' said Mick laughing.

Chapter 5

Back at the house, Charlie laid out the maps on the lounge carpet. The three boys knelt down looking at them. Charlie pointed out, 'This is the building work to be carried out, and this is another map of the construction and placement of the vault. But this map here is the important one. It is the area map and location part of the town and surrounding area.'

They spent a couple of hours debating and pondering over and over about the rebuild of the holding centre bank. The details of the bank vault were the most important details they had to learn. The layers of concrete and the reinforcing steel all had to be calculated.

'It looks like the floor of the vault will be three feet thick with two-inch reinforcing bars.'

'What we will do is this,' said Charlie, 'as they build the bank, we will dig a Tunnel from the derelict house that we purchase across the road. We will pretend to be renovating the house but we will be actually digging the Tunnel from inside the derelict house underneath the road across to the bank. We will visit the bank the night they put in the mass concrete for the vault. We will make alterations to the floor to make it easier for us to come in underneath when it's full of cash.'

'Fuck me,' said Billy, 'when are we going to start the Tunnel.'

'Look at this street map across the road. There are two old three-storey rundown derelict buildings and are for sale. Thirty grand each will buy the two of them from the council.'

'Thirty grand,' said Billy, 'for each three-storey building.'

'Yes,' said Charlie, 'because the council wants to get investors in to turn them into new shops, that is why they are so cheap.'

'And you, Mick, will be the purchasing agent in a few weeks. So we must get you a completely new identity.'

'So in the daytime we will be cleaning out the ground floor down to the cellar preparing for the Tunnel across the road while the builders are building the bank.'

'Nice one,' said Billy, 'no one will take notice of us renovating the old buildings for the new shops.'

'But we will be removing the flooring over the sellers. Get our equipment down,' said Mick.

'Right,' said Charlie, 'that is the plan. We have a lot of work to do but we must get money very soon to finance this job. You must buy the property in a false name so that's money down the drain if we don't succeed in our bank job. Also, we must get all measurements right. We must go into the bank and insert a steel rod into the ground inside the bank vault door area as soon as the foundation stone trunking is put in. We will enter that night.'

'So how will we get through the three-foot concrete and reinforcing?' asked Mick.

'We would go in at night time and make changes. The night they pour the concrete, before it dries we go in and remove a square yard cube.'

Chapter 6

'We will cut the rebar and remove one square yard of concrete and reinforcement from the vault foundation concrete that was poured earlier in the day. We would position our entry to the vault just inside the vault door. That way nothing will be on top of entry hole.'

'I see it here on the map. When we take out the square yard and remove the rebar, we will then have a cube box same side to put down into the floor of the vault. Before we put the box in place, we will hammer down a six feet steel rod in the centre of the box down into the ground. That rod when we find it in our Tunnel, we will then know we are in the centre of the box that we have to remove to gain entry to the floor of the vault. When the box is in place, we will put three inches of concrete back on top of the vault floor and re-float the floor again so that nobody will know we were in. The box will have no bottom. So when we find the rod in the Tunnel, we clean out the ground around the rod. What we have to do is jack away the tree inches of concrete above the box with a hydraulic jack that will snap the whole square of concrete out in one go. It will be like pushing out a piece of the jigsaw. It will snap like a piece of glass as it has no reinforcing in it. The square of slab of concrete we jack up like a shore cover.'

'What happens Charlie if the alarm goes off when we jack up the floor? Can they get into the vault and catch us in the act?'

'No,' said Charlie, 'the time locks will keep them out for some time. Also the minute we get in, we attach a chain to the door on the inside. We will pull that chain with a five-ton pulley blocks, so they can't get in even if they override the time locks. The only way of getting in is through the wall.

They will not know what is wrong with the door, and why it won't open. This will give us lots of time to empty the vault through the Tunnel. We will also hang a black curtain from the ceiling of the vault one foot away from the inside walls so that if they drill a hole in the wall to put in a fish lens camera to see what is going on, all they will see is black. This will give us lots of time to get away and hide all our cash and tidy up loose ends. I envisage we will be finished and gone home two days before they gain entry to the vault.'

Chapter 7

'Now you men must move down here next week and keep a low profile in this town,' Charlie said.

Billy said, 'There was a big robbery of a vault in Northern Ireland some time ago and thirty million was stolen in that robbery. And the government cancelled the launch of the new currency and reprinted a different design, this fucked up the robbery. That fact alone proves it was not an inside job. If it was inside, someone fucked up. Those Irish guys should have known about that and waited a few months.'

'Okay,' Charlie. 'So we must make sure they are not launching a new currency at the time we are doing the robbery?'

'Correct.'

'That is a good point. Billy, remind me do some research to make sure no new currencies are about to be launched, otherwise we will have a lot of paper to burn just like the Irish guys had.'

'I wouldn't worry too much about that, you may be sure we will find millions in old use notes. And also, I bet we will find a lot of foreign currency.'

'Nice one,' says Billy, 'just might visit every country to spend their money.'

'Are we taking coins?' said Mick with a laugh.

'Them millions can stay where it is,' said Charlie.

'It's only small change,' said Billy laughing.

'It appears to me,' Charlie said, 'Mick, that you seem to know a lot more about the contents of that vault, and it's not even built yet.'

'Let's say I was told a secret.'

Billy got serious and said, 'Charlie, are we mad or very clever. This will be the biggest cash robbery ever carried out in the world.'

'To get away with it is the clever bit.'

'So now I told you,' said Charlie, 'have you any questions to ask?'

Billy said, 'Mick what you think?'

'Well, I'm in.'

'The pay is good, so am I,' said Billy.

'But how the fuck will we count this money?' said Mick. 'I never counted the proceeds of any bank that I rob.'

'The bank will tell you how much you stole on the TV,' said Charlie. 'We have a lot of work to do, and I'm off to bed. I am mentally tired. Plenty of drink in the fridge, boys, if you want it,' said Charlie as he walked up the stairs. 'If you come up with any ideas let me know in the morning.'

Charlie was still talking from the bedroom. He said, 'I will make a list of all the tools and equipment we need for this piece of work. We will have to count everything before and after the job in case we lose one of our bits. O'Brien's, we leave behind us,' said Charlie walking back down the stairs to continue talking. 'We will be leaving all the equipment and tools on site that is O'Brien's. But we will have to make sure that we don't leave any forensic evidence behind.'

Charlie went up the stairs and went to bed. 8 am, Saturday morning, Charlie was up and out of bed. Nobody was out of bed, only him. Charlie walked into the spare room, 'Right, lads, out of bed. Go home and prepare to move down here in the next week. I'm going to collect the kids and do some shopping. I will call you so take care for now.'

Driving around town, Charlie decided to have a look in the bank windows as if the kids were asking Daddy to show them what was in the bank where Daddy used to get his money.

The child said, 'The bank is closed forever and the bank man is gone away with all your money. Won't be able to get new toys anymore?'

'No, son, the bank man is up the road in a new building for a little while because they are building a new bank inside this old one.'

'Will they bring back all your money, Daddy?' said his little girl.

'Yes, my princess, they will bring it all back but we can go to the other bank to get some now. And we go get some toys.'

'Can we get new bicycles for Christmas, Daddy?' asked Ellie Mai.

'Of course, you can, and any other present you want. Because I love you two, you're the best in the world.'

'I won't have to cycle my old rusty bike anymore,' asked Jerome.

'No, you will not.'

'Can I get a Barbie doll today, Daddy?'

'Yes, Ellie, you can.' Charlie had a good look around the bank and in the windows while he was talking to the kids as if he was showing the kids what was going on with the new build. The bank was now a couple of weeks into the build, and it was cleared out inside. Next month, they will have the roof off and the floors out so they must get working fast. They had already made plans to purchase the derelict buildings across the road, the sale would be through next week as they were a cash buyer. The new ID went down a treat with the estate agent, and the deal was going through. Next week they would get into the derelict house on a caretaker's agreement while the sale was going through. And every Saturday they would check the progress of the bank.

Chapter 8

A couple of days passed, and Charlie spent some time in his workshop at the back of the house designing the box to insert into the vault floor. The box that Charlies built had no bottom so that when they Tunnel up to it, they would be inside the box and all that would be above them would be the tree inches of concrete they put on top of the box. When the box was inserted into the floor, they placed a tripod on top of the box with a telescopic pole on it. Attached to the top of the pole was a laser level that shone through the bank window and continued to shine through the derelict window where the spot on the wall of the derelict house was. Billy was be at the derelict house with a felt pen to mark an X at the spot on the wall and continued over to the glass window and put in another X where the laser beam came through the glass, as this gave an angle to where the box was.

When they dropped a plumb line from the X on the wall and the plumb line from the X on the glass, it gave them an angle of trajectory in the cellar where they placed a laser beam on the cellar wall shining at the same angle of the measurement; it was hundred and fifty feet from the spot on the wall to where the rebar was hammered down under the box. They Tunnelled at that angle with the hundred and fifty feet with the laser shining on the Tunnel face at all times as they worked, they couldn't go wrong then.

Two weeks passed since they were in the town Hall and Charlie had been very busy working out what was to be done. Charlie had all the tools and equipment listed to do the job. Mick and Billy moved into a house offside. The rules were to keep a low profile at all times, no talking in the pub about the job. From now on, they drank in McCarthy's pub most of the time. McCarthy's is an international pub. Lots of outsiders drink in there. This pub had a beer garden where they could have private conversations without anybody listening to them.

Friday night came again. Charlie, Billy and Mick went to the beer garden in McCarthy's.

'Right, lads, the bank is gutted inside, it's time we start. We now have a caretaker's agreement while the sale of the property is going through because we handed over the full money for the purchase to the vendor's solicitors. We can get to work. We have a few other things to do. Tomorrow is Saturday and I have borrowed a digger. We are going outside the town to dig a hole to bury a diesel tank that we have acquired. Actually, lads, the bad news is we have to bury two of them.'

'What is this all about?' asked Billy.

'You will know in good time,' said Charlie. 'We must bury the two tanks tomorrow. One is to stash the cash and the other is to stash the trash, for example all the labels from the money and the moneybags. In a few days' time, we will be starting to dig the Tunnel. In the meantime, we must go to O'Brien the builders to get all the equipment we need to dig that Tunnel. We need them little railway tracks with the dirt bins on wheels. We will also need an electric heist to lift the bin out of the cellar and have them emptied out the back of the derelict houses, and we will also have to put some of the dirt in the cellar of the old house next door. We will need acro props to prop up the Tunnel.'

'The best thing,' said Mick, 'is to explain everything as we go along.'

'Okay,' said Charlie. 'I am only thinking out loud trying to work out every detail.'

Chapter 9

The next morning, Charlie, Billy and Mick were out early. Charlie got a digger and were are out the country in a secluded place, digging the hole for a 1000-gallon plastic diesel tank which Charlie had on a trailer. After about an hour Charlie said to Billy, 'It's deep enough, tie on the tank to the bucket of the digger with that rope.'

Charlie lifted the tank down into the hole in the ground and quickly buried it and pushed away all the extra soil that he dug up and pulled back the bushes that he pushed away before he started the dig, to camouflage the tank area. The top of the tank was changed. It had a hatch on it so that they could climb down into it. When the tank was buried, they went back to the yard and got a new tank for the next hole and they did the same thing again at the other end of the town.

'Why do we have two tanks?' asked Mick.

'One for the money and one for the trash,' said Charlie.

'You're asking technical questions now, Mick,' said Billy.

'It's going to take the three of us to do this job, and the more I explain and you understand, the more you can to carry it out.'

Later that night Charlie, Billy and Mick met to break into O'Brien's the builders to get the equipment. In the yard, Charlie had a list of equipment they needed. A jackhammer, electric type steel rod for the floor of vault angle grinder 200 acro props. Two miniature rail carriages and two hundred feet of rail track. Twenty-ton hydraulic jack. Two hundred scaffolding planks to prop up the Tunnel. Flood lighting. Four shovels, two pick axes, six ft. crowbar. Billy said to Charlie,

'Everything we need is here in O'Brien's yard. Load all the stuff into the trailer and a big van and we'll borrow them.'

'I will get the key in O'Brien's office. You come with me, Billy.'

They went into the office to get the keys for the vans to take the stuff. 'We bring the van and trailer back tonight. You stay there, Mick, and keep a lookout.'

Charlie and Billy went into O'Brien's office. In the office Charlie was searching the drawers and found the key and then he searched a filing cabinet and took out the planning permission granted to him to do the bank. Charlie opened the envelope and took out the map of the surrounding area and with a biro he marked very small pin hole on the map.

'What are you doing Charlie?' said Billy,

They put the map back in the envelope and returned it to the draw where he got it. 'All in good time, Billy, all in good time.'

It was late when Charlie, Billy and Mick were finished that night. They put all the equipment into the derelict house. The bank was now a month into the renovations. The old shop floor across the road was prepared for the dig, and the laser projection on the wall. That Monday night Charlie, Billy and Mick climbed over the hoarding board that builders erected at the bank. They measured the area of the vault that was being prepared for concrete and rebar. They picked the spot and hammered down a six-foot steel rod into the ground until it could not be seen anymore, then they left the bank.

Charlie said that they will pour the concrete this week for the vault. 'We better be ready for that.'

Every day in Charlie's workshop at the back of the house, they went over and over the plan and the progress they were making. Charlie said to Billy, 'We need some finances. We have no more money left to spend on this job. Do you have anything in mind that we could do to get some money?'

'No problem, we just hit a few banks.'

'I'm not into that running in to a bank without planning it,' said Charlie.

'Me too,' said Mick.

'Well, we just plan one then.'

'I just thought of something,' said Mick.

'What is on your mind?' said Charlie to Mick.

'I met a bird who works in a bank but if you think I am going to go with this one no way. She is coyote ugly.'

'Just introduce her to me,' said Billy.

'I will get the information we need. If we go to Jacksonvilla nightclub next Friday night, it's guaranteed that she will be there hoping that a man would turn up to dance with her,' said Mick.

'You and Billy will go to Jacksonvilla nightclub next Friday night and get everything out of her brain about the security systems in that bank and where the money is. When it is. Everything.'

'Leave it to me,' said Billy. 'She will fall in love with me and tell me everything. I will tell her she is beautiful.'

'She will know you are lying,' said Mick.

'Maybe she will,' said Billy, 'but she will love the sound of them words in her ear.'

That Friday night, Billy and Mick were at the nightclub early and just like Mick said she was there on her own waiting for her knight in shining armour.

Chapter 10

Charlie called into Mick and Billy to have a chat about getting some finances to continue their project in the Tunnel. 'Right, boys,' Charlie said, 'you have had a few weeks to go to Jacksonvilla and talk to that woman that you know who works in the bank up the other end of the country. So what's the position on that now?'

Billy said, 'I went to the nightclub, and I danced with her all night and took her back to the hotel we were staying in. Can you fucking believe it, she was playing fucking hard to get. Anyway, I told her she was beautiful but she was having none of it so I went back a few nights, and she started to loosen up. She told me she works in the counting room at the back of the bank every Monday, and the back door is left open for fresh air but there's no way in only over the twenty-foot wall so they feel secure. She doesn't suspect that I intend to come in that back door and relieve her of her bags of cash.'

'So, Billy, when are ye to go to rob a few bags of that cash we really need?'

'Next Monday morning at ten o'clock, we will go down the back lane in a van with a double ladder on top, one part of the ladder for each side of the wall.'

'Okay, let's get it done.'

'I will drive the van,' said Charlie, 'ye two go in over the wall and get what you can.'

Monday morning, at five o'clock, the three boys were in the van with double ladders on the roof. They drove to the town at the other end of the country. They waited till 9:45. They had their boiler suits, ski masks and gloves on; they didn't need guns for this bank robbery. They were only slipping in the back door and grabbing the bags off the floor, no need to frighten Billy's new girlfriend.

At ten o'clock on the dot, they drove down the lane behind the bank and erected one ladder up the wall and the second ladder on the inside. Billy and Mick quickly scaled the ladder and down into the yard of the bank running in the back door. Billy's girlfriend was counting the money just like she said she would. They grabbed two bags each off the floor, and they quickly scaled back out into the lane and into the van and away. They quickly changed cars and got rid of their boiler suits, gloves and ski masks. They were back home in their own house by 1 pm counting the money. They now had two hundred grand to finance the Tunnel project.

'That was easy,' said Mick.

'Yes, I know,' Billy said.

'Too many things can go wrong with them bank jobs. Cops in the wrong place at the wrong time,' said Charlie. 'Get some rest, lads, we will go out tonight for a few drinks.

The next day the three of them worked in the derelict house until late in the afternoon.

*

Billy came running into Charlie's house. 'Come on,' he said, 'we must get down to the bank, the concrete trucks are outside, we must have a look at where they are pouring it. I looked over the hoarding boards to see the men are walking in the vault area preparing for the cement. I saw them doing the last tie offs on the reinforcement bars.'

*

'Right, lads,' said Charlie, 'this is where it begins, it looks like the vault floor is going in today and it's four o'clock now so they will be working late to pour this concrete, that's good for us. The minute they leave we will go in and remove the three square feet cube and remove the rebar.'

The builders were finished at 7:30 pm. It was just getting dark and Charlie, Billy and Mick were going over the hoarding in a secluded part, where nobody could see them. All the tools they needed were on the site.

'Quickly,' said Charlie, 'get an extension lead plugged in to run the angle grinder. Billy, you help me to measure out the floor to find the spot where we put down the steel rod a couple weeks ago.' Charlie and Billy measured the floor and found the spot, they had the cube box Charlie made in the shed with them. Charlie and Billy scooped out the wet concrete and came upon lots of two-inch reinforcement bars in the cement. Mick had the angle grinder ready to cut the bars one by one as Charlie and Billy kept scooping out the concrete. Eventually the cube was ready to be inserted into the ground, and they could see that the steel rod was still there hammered into the ground in the centre of the box. Billy and Mick lifted the box down into the ground, and Charlie levelled it up, and measured to see if they had three inches above the box for the concrete to go on top.

'It's correct,' said Charlie, 'fill in the cement all around the box and on top.' Quickly the three of them filled in the wet cement and back to where it was on top of the box. They got down on their knees and floated the cement into place then they through a bucket of water all over the vault and the three of them used floating trowels to re-float the whole floor to blend in where they had dug out. They were in there two hours and the job was done.

'Perfect,' said Charlie, 'they will never know we were in. We must get rid of all the rebar, we will bury it where they'll never find it in a corner over there.' Looking at their handiwork they were impressed that you wouldn't notice that someone had gone in there and re floated that floor. The boys were leaving with the sweat running down their faces from working so quickly.

'I was at a little bit scared of getting caught inside.'

'That went like clockwork,' said Charlie to the two boys.

When they left the bank, Charlie said, 'We must be upstairs in the derelict house in the morning with strong binoculars as the men come in to work on the vault. We will know by their actions, if they notice anything different about the concrete floor of the vault.'

Chapter 11

After they finished working on the bank vault floor, they went home for a wash. Then they went to the pub.

'That went like clockwork, Charlie,' Mick said.

'I agree,' said Billy.

'What are you going to do with the money?' said Mick to Charlie.

'We will invest the cash into property. But let's worry about getting the money first. We have worried all our lives about getting money without getting caught. So that will change,' continued Charlie. 'So money will always be on your mind one way or another. So it just changes to a different kind of worry.'

'At least it will be happy worry,' said Billy laughing.

'No,' said Charlie, 'worrying about losing it is worse than worrying about getting it. You will have a lot of sleepless nights worrying about some cunt finding our fucking money and fucking robbing us. I lost millions before, Billy.' Charlie looked at the boys and said, 'but not this time, boys, not this fucking time.'

Marilyn was out for the night and was on the lookout for Charlie in the pubs because they were together in secret last week. They had a wild sex and if Celine found out Charlie would be history with her. Celine and her sister Zola were in McCarthy's pub as well.

'This is not good,' said Charlie. Charlie's personal life and relationships with women was very complicated. He wouldn't have it any other way. It was his second occupation. Marilyn was with her two good-looking girlfriends.

Marilyn said to her friend Catherine, 'I met a guy last week called Charlie, a really nice guy. I really like him. He is living in a courtyard about five miles outside town. It is the most beautiful place you could imagine. But it is a bit spooky out there at night time.'

'Does that guy you're talking about have a silver Mitsubishi Warrior jeep?' asked Catherine.

'Yes,' said Marilyn.

'Who are you talking about?' asked Marilyn's other friend Fiona.

'Nobody,' said Marilyn wanting to keep Charlie a secret for now.

Fiona said, 'That guy is hooked up with that posh Jewish bitch Celine Dayoni. Stay away from him, Jane.'

Marilyn put her head down in shame, thinking of what she did last week with Charlie. She knew now that Charlie used her like a rag doll for fun. She let Charlie shag her like she was getting paid for the night. What a fool she felt being Charlie's whore.

Billy came back from the pub toilet and said, 'Charlie, I've just seen Marilyn in the back area with two beautiful women and guess what? Celine is not far away from them.'

'So we better back off out the door, and come back later,' said Charlie. 'It's too dangerous to go down around them with Celine close by.'

'I am not listening to you and Celine fighting if she sees you talking to Marilyn,' said Mick.

'You're talking sense, Mick, let's get out of here before we are spotted by them.'

On the way out the door, Charlie said, 'Remember my friends – never tell a woman a secret that would put you in jail. Because that is where you will be going when she catches you shagging another bird.'

'So what do you talk about in bed with your lover?' Mick said to Charlie.

'It's like this,' replied Charlie. 'All every woman wants to hear in bed is how beautiful she is, and how good she is in bed so that will keep you busy forever. Always tell a woman how beautiful she is as she walks out the door with you in hand.

Nothing else matters more to the female species than told they are beautiful.'

Charlie continued his speech in the next pub. 'I tell you, my friends. If a man puts a coin in a jar every time, he makes love to his new girlfriend for the first year. And then take a coin out of the jar every time, he makes love the second year. What will they have in the jar at the beginning of the third year?'

'Don't know,' said Billy.

'Don't know,' said Mick.

'Think about it,' says Charlie. 'Put a coin in the jar every time he made love to his new girlfriend the first year. So the jar is full. Every time, he makes love to his new girlfriend the second year he takes a coin out of the jar. How much is in the jar in the third year? The answer is,' said Charlie, 'the third year he would still have a jar full of coins.'

Billy and Mick looked at Charlie and by their faces Charlie knew they still didn't get it.

Charlie said, 'Think about it later, boys.'

When Billy went to the toilet, Mick asked Charlie what was the answer. 'Tell me before Billy comes back.'

Charlie said, 'He filled the jar with coins the first year because he made love three times a day.

He didn't make love the second year – it was all sex so the jar stayed full trigger, my old friend.'

Billy came back from the toilet and said, 'Charlie, I know the answer – the jar was full because he didn't it make love in the second year.'

'You're right, Billy.'

'Well, Charlie,' said Mick. 'My motto is. Find them. Fuck them, and forget them. The three Fs.'

Billy said, 'It is a poor mouse that has only one hole to run into. When you fight with the girlfriend run and make love to the bit on the side. That will cure you.'

Charlie said, 'Remember, boys, when you are in prison all them women will do on Friday night what you did every Friday night when you are out. Just like last Friday night. So don't feel sorry for them now. Because they will not feel sorry for you then.'

Chapter 12

Over the weekend Charlie, Billy and Mick moved all the equipment they collected from O'Brien the builder's yard into the derelict building across the road from the bank. They were now working on the start of the Tunnel. They dropped the plumb line down from the two laser spots: one on the wall and one on the glass of the window. They dropped down to the cellar floor. They then mounted a laser under the drop from the wall. They pointed the laser from the wall drop to the window drop line; it gave the angle that the Tunnel must be dug at.

The laser was now shining on the wall that was their centre point. They worked the Tunnel six feet high by six foot wide. From the centre of the laser spot is three feet on every direction which gives you the square of the Tunnel. The laser must remain in the same position for the duration of the dig and must not be moved at any time. To recalibrate the laser you have to drop the plumb line from the window spot to the basement floor and shine the laser on the drop line from where it was mounted on the back wall.

Sunday night Charlie, Billy and Mick entered the bank building site to check on the floor and to see if anything was noticed.

'The floor of the vault is lovely and hard as a rock,' said Mick. They walked on the concrete where the box was to see if they could hear a hollow sound, but they couldn't. The next morning at 8 am, Charlie, Billy and Mick went to work in the derelict house across the road. All the workers in the bank were hard at the renovations. By 10 am, they had the first two feet of Tunnel dug out and the acro prop were in place holding up the roof of the Tunnel with the two scaffolding planks. The acros were jacked up pushing the planks up into the mud to carry the weight of the road.

*

Charlie, Billy and Mick were out of bed again at 8 am, going to work. They had to remove all the soil they had piled up in the basement of the old house. At the dig site Charlie and Mick were shovelling clay into the big bins they had down in the basement and Billy was above hoisting the bins and unloading them into the basement at the backroom of the house. They were now four feet into the Tunnel and must lay down their little rail track to shovel the rubble into the bins. Billy got his first length of rail track and put it underground from the centre of the basement four feet into the Tunnel.

'We now have the Tunnel cleaned out,' said Charlie, 'and all the rubble is gone so we can now start digging again.' They worked hard to get another two feet of the Tunnel dug out and propped with the acro props and scaffolding planks across them. Charlie and Billy rigged up a light strip for the Tunnel as it was getting dark in there. They were now eight feet into the Tunnel.

'Let's finish for the day,' said Charlie, 'and go and have a few drinks as we have earned them.'

In the pub Billy said, 'We have not come across any rock yet.'

'I don't expect to meet any rock,' said Charlie.

'Don't worry about it, Billy. If we do, as we'll take it out as well. If we do this type of hard work every day it will drain us very quickly so we must take some time off because we have months to finish this Tunnel,' said Charlie.

Mick said, 'I don't mind the hard work as the pay will be good.'

'We have a lot to take care of,' said Billy.

'I know, boys,' said Charlie, 'we will cross every bridge when we come to it no matter what. We will take tomorrow off. I have to go and see Joseph about his new house build.'

*

Charlie had some free time so he went and met Joseph at the new house building site. It didn't take Charlie long to see that Joseph was right when he said O'Brien the builders were ripping him off in every way they could. And it seemed legally Joseph can't do anything about it.

'Well, you can't, Joseph, but I can,' said Charlie. Charlie phoned O'Brien the builders to arrange a meeting with the boss robber for that afternoon. At the meeting Mr O'Brien said, 'How can I help you, Charlie?'

'It's about my father-in-law's house you are building. I was out there this morning, and I can see what is going on. Mr O'Brien, you are robbing my father-in-law.'

'Why can't he come and see me himself, and we sort out any problems or issues he has on our building work?'

'I will tell you, Mr O'Brien. He is so upset he doesn't have the strength to come and argue his case, that is why I am here for him.' Charlie took up his briefcase and put on the table.

'Don't tell me you have some court papers for me?'

'I don't,' said Charlie opening the briefcase. 'No, I just have this.' Opening the case he took out a large size ballpoint hammer and put it to O'Brien's head. 'You won't be going to any court if you don't sort out. Finish the rest of Joseph's house and also give him back the money you overcharged him. If you continue to rob my father-in-law, you will have so much brain damage from this brand-new hammer, your wife won't recognise you.

'What do you want me to do, Charlie – I will do it.'

'Just lift the phone and call Joseph and tell him that you will replace all the cheap plumbing and wiring you put into his house in the last month.'

'I will do it straight away.'

Charlie was leaving the room with his briefcase when he turned and said. 'Mr O'Brien, you should have plenty of money from robbing the National bank building contract.'

Mr O'Brien did not see Charlie take the business card of his desk which read "O'Brien the builders, the honest builders". The card had fingerprints on it in cement.

Charlie, Billy and Mick went into the bank building site for one last look. The box was situated near the door entrance to the vault, as they did not want any heavy boxes on top of the entrance hatch that will come up through. The vault was nearly built, everything looked in the right place look at the thickness of them walls. Charlie picked up a piece of old reinforcement bar, he laid on the ground and put his ear to the floor. He then used the piece of rebar to tap the floor and see if he got a hollow sound now that all the concrete was dry and rock hard.

Billy joined Charlie and put his ear to the ground. Charlie tapped the floor again.

Billy said, 'I can hear the hollow, Charlie.'

'So can I.'

Charlie had one more look around before they left the bank building site for the last time. Billy turned around and said to Charlie and Mick, 'Lads, the next time we walk on this ground we will go down in history for all time.'

Mick said laughing out loud, 'For the biggest spud robbery the world have ever seen.'

Back at the derelict buildings, the pressure was on now to get this Tunnel completed.

Billy said, 'We are only about ten feet into the Tunnel so we have a long way to go.'

'But we have months left,' said Charlie.

'I know that, Billy, but we could run into problems so the quicker we get the Tunnel built the better, and we can just close it up and wait for the right time.'

'Billy said we must recalibrate the laser in case we bump off it when working.'

'Good thinking,' said Charlie. 'If the laser is out of place, we will pass by the steel rod that show us where the box is. Billy, you and Mick recalibrate that laser now with the plumb lines just to make sure we don't forget.'

Charlie, Billy and Mick were tired as they were digging for hours every day to get the Tunnel finished. They dig away one foot from the Tunnel face. Then they put a plank across the two acro props, jack them up into the mud above with great pressure to make sure each one was carrying its own weight. The little railway track was making the job very easy. They wheeled in the little carriage on the tracks, and load it up with clay and stones from the dig and wheel it out. They hooked the carriage onto the electric hoist chain that hung down from above it which was secured to the ceiling and roof.

Billy was above controlling the hoist, lifting the bins one by one. He pulled them onto the ground and wheeled them out to empty them out. This was going on for some weeks, and they were nearly half way into the Tunnel. Billy recalibrated the laser every morning to make sure they were going straight for the steel rod under the box. They had to finish the whole Tunnel before the security alarm company installed the sensor equipment in the bank floors, and especially the vault.

Chapter 13

As they finished up for the day Billy said, 'The place is nice and tidy so we will block up the Tunnel wall with them sheets of plywood so that if anybody comes snooping into our building site, they will not see the Tunnel.'

'Good thinking,' said Charlie. 'Let's put up the sheeting across the whole wall.'

'Also,' said Billy, 'We must not make friends with them builders in the bank. That will only entice them to visit our building site to see how we are getting on.'

'I don't talk to any of them migrant builders,' said Mick.

Charlie said, 'They are nice people. They will help you out, if you were stuck. When I see them on the streets, I turn my head away. I am very impressed with the way both of you are using your brains on this project. I really appreciate it that I don't have to think of everything.'

Mick said, 'Charlie, I didn't want to say it but I thought you knew we need more acro props?'

'It slipped my mind, Mick. We will go to O'Brien's yard as he has thousands of them. Mick, estimate how many more we need.'

'I have already done that – we had two hundred to be on the safe side, and we need another one hundred.'

'Okay, Mick, we will get them later tonight. Do we need any other equipment that I have not thought about?'

'We need the hundred tonne jack,' said Billy.

'We got that,' said Charlie. 'I think it's in my yard.'

'I will check, tonight,' said Billy, 'before we go for the acro props.'

Charlie continued, 'Billy, would it not be a good idea that when we are finished with work every evening, we put every piece of our equipment into the Tunnel before we put up the false wall?'

'Do you know what, Billy, you're starting to think just like me, and so are you, Mick. It's a pleasure to work with both of you.'

Charlie was home alone when Celine and her father came in the door to have a few drinks. When he had a chance, Joseph said to Charlie in the kitchen when he got him on his own, 'O'Brien the builder sorted out my house this week, and he said I don't owe him any more money. He told me you called to see him with a hammer. What did you say to him?'

'I told him you sent me down to the hardware shop to get you a new ballpoint hammer that you were going to kill O'Brien with. So I said to him that I talked you out of doing anything and that you were very volatile and unpredictable so we better sort it out now. I showed him your new hammer.'

Joseph was thriving on the conversation of violence when in fact he was a really gentle man.

*

People like me should always be protected from scumbag builders like O'Brien. Joseph said, 'Again I bet that O'Brien is robbing the bank with his bills for the shoddy work that they are carrying out. I'd say he will charge the bank double the price for what it really would cost. I bet some backhanders were paid to them councillors, and the bank manager to give the contract to O'Brien builders.'

Charlie's ears were wide open but not a word did he have to say about that bank build. If Celine and her innocent father only knew how hard Charlie's building work was this week, and the bank will pay a lot more than O'Brien's.

Billy and Mick were relaxing in the house they had offside. They were both very quiet; they each knew that the Tunnel and the bank was on their minds. They were trying to imagine what it was like to see all that cash in that vault.

Celine didn't ask Charlie about his business, she knew he had some property and he had an income from the rental of his property. Celine didn't need Charlie for money as they are a wealthy Jewish family that dealt in diamonds. They also had very strict Jewish rules. Celine drove a top of the range Mercedes G wagon that her father gave her for her birthday last year. She didn't need him for money. Charlie was very much in love with Celine, and his biggest fear was to get caught, not at the bank, but with another woman in his bed.

*

It was 8 am, and Charlie was at the derelict building for another full day's work in the Tunnel. Upon arriving at the worksite Billy and Mick were already there and had removed the false wall hiding their Tunnel and minding their tools. Charlie did his morning check on every acro prop.

Billy said, 'I noticed that some of them props are loose because the floor is turning into mud.'

'Yes, you are right, Billy,' said Charlie. 'I will use this six-inch solid cement building block out the back. I will spend the day removing each prop one by one and placing them in a cement block to spread the weight in the mud.' So Charlie worked all day inserting the solid cement blocks under every acro and re-jacked every acro into the roof of the Tunnel, and this made it very strong. Billy and Mick had added a new link of the rail track to the floor of the Tunnel.

They had got from O'Brien's yard the extra one hundred acro props. People could hear the work being carried out in the derelict buildings but they ignored it because they were just renovating, just like the noise coming from the renovations at the bank across the road. Charlie put a whiteboard across the face of the Tunnel, and Billy recalibrated the laser direction. The measured from the spot on the wall to the face of the Tunnel and did their calculations to find that they were totally accurate.

'How far more?' asked Mick as he was laying out the string of lights to put more light in the Tunnel.'

'According to my calculations, we are under the vault but we have to get to the other end of the vault where we will meet the steel rod under the box.'

'How accurate do you think the laser is?' said Billy.

'Well, it's like this,' said Charlie. 'I expect that laser to shine on our rod.'

'I bet you a bag of spuds Billy that the laser will shine on the road,' said Mick.

'No way,' said Billy.

'I can feel the vibrations from the traffic driving past over our heads,' said Charlie.

'We are feeling that all this week,' said Mick. 'We are months at this Tunnel now. We will be at the box in the next two weeks.'

Billy said to Charlie, 'I will check the road above us and see have we got any hairline cracks.'

'Good thinking,' said Charlie.

Chapter 14

O'Brien the builders finished off the roof of the bank so all the heavy work must be completed inside. The painters would be moving in in about two weeks they were only about six feet away from the rod and the box.

'We could do an overnight shift digging out the rest of the Tunnel,' said Mick.

'No,' said Charlie. 'We don't want to attract any attention from anybody. Because we're so deep into the Tunnel nobody can hear us work anymore. And we are not using any power tools. We will finish up early today, we have worked very hard the last few weeks. We need to take a night out and let off some steam.'

In the pub that night during conversation Mick said, 'Is there anything we might have forgotten to take into account?'

'There is one thing on my mind,' said Billy.

'What is that?' asked Charlie.

'What if we got very heavy rain will?'

'The Tunnel will flood,' said Charlie.

'What can we prepare for that?'

'How about digging a square in the basement floor lower than the Tunnel floor so that any water that comes in the Tunnel will fill the square first. And in the hole, we place an electric powered drop pump the minute we see water. The pump would pump it out the back of the building and down into the drains.'

'Okay, Charlie, we will sort that tomorrow and get a drop pump into position. Then the drop pumps would remove huge amounts of water like a fire hose. And also the drop pump makes no noise when it is submerged in water. So we can leave it on all night. We will go to the tool hire shop, and I will hire out a lawnmower. I will have the jeep near the drop pumps in the yard. You and Billy get the biggest drop pump in the back of the jeep and don't get caught taking it.'

The next morning the three of them went to the tool hire yard. Charlie hired out the lawnmower and Billy and Mick got a good drop pump. On the way back to the derelict building, Charlie said, 'We may not need it but it's better to have it just in case.'

Saturday morning it rained very heavy and Charlie got out of bed at 9 am and went to the derelict building. Billy was already there. 'Any water?' asked Charlie.

'Not a drop,' said Billy, 'the whole Tunnel is now dry.'

'Thanks, Billy, for getting up early to check out the Tunnel for water. It's Saturday. You and Mick meet me tonight in McCarthy's at 7 pm.'

'Okay, Charlie, we will be there.'

*

Charlie could see Marilyn all dolled up to the nines. Charlie was taking a lot of chances meeting Marilyn behind Celine's back. Mick said to Charlie, 'Why are you risking getting caught by Celine for Marilyn?'

'I don't know,' said Charlie, 'must be the challenge or the chase to see can I get Marilyn into my bed.'

'Well, if Celine finds out you will be history with her.'

'Anyway,' said Billy, 'myself and Mick carried out checks on the road every evening looking for hairline cracks.'

'I know that you and Mick are well on top of this project. And also thanks Billy for going in this morning checking the rain hadn't come in and flood the place.' Charlie was very impressed with his two men and the way they were conducting themselves in this serious project. And also in the way they were keeping a very low profile. Nobody seemed to see them around except on the weekends in McCarthy's pub.

Charlie told the boys, 'I went to the two diesel tank hideouts and checked to see if they have blended back in with the shrubs. Everything is perfect. The two tanks have a hatch door and a small ladder inside. I climbed under the bush today and used a small panel saw to cut the sod on top of the hatch so the hatch lifts up with the sod on top of it. I had a quick look in to see if it was all dry inside. And it was. There is no condensation or anything inside them tanks, they are a perfect hideout. But just in case, we get condensation I put in a bag of white polystyrene bedding. This will absorb any damp inside. Polystyrene molecules have a natural heat in them that will keep the tanks dry.'

'Okay, boys,' said Charlie, 'let's head to the nightclub. I am meeting Celine upstairs.'

Mick said to Charlie, 'Is that one of the O'Brien builders over there at the bar?'

Billy interrupted and said, 'It is.'

'Did he spot any of us on site, do you think?'

'No,' said Charlie and Mick.

Charlie said, 'I will talk to him and find out how the bank build is going.' Charlie made his way to the bar where the builder was standing and ordered another round. Charlie got talking to the builder and said to him, 'You are the policeman that caught me speeding on the motorway last week and done me for it. I was only two miles over the speed limit, and you still gave me the ticket.'

'You're mistaken mister, I am a builder working on the bank down the road for O'Brien's.'

The builder lifted up his beer and Charlie said, 'Sorry about that, looking at the size of your hands, you are definitely a builder. I will get you a drink for being so stupid and calling you a cop.'

'Okay, mate, I will have a beer. My name is Meric and I am from Moscow. I am building the bank down the road with O'Brien the builders.'

'So you are building the bank down the road? Will it be long more before it's open?'

'About six weeks.'

'I thought that bank had gone bust and closed down over the recession?'

'No, they are building a new bank inside and retaining the four old facet walls.'

'So when will the new bank be opened then for business?'

'It will be open in about six weeks,' said the builder.

Now that Charlie got the same answer twice: six weeks. He needed to make a quick exit. 'I better find my girlfriend,' said Charlie walking away from the builder. Back at the table where the builder could not see them, Charlie told Billy and Mick, 'I was talking to the builder, and he said the bank would be finished in six weeks. So tomorrow we will finish the Tunnel as we don't have far to go. This means the bank will be finished quicker than I estimated. And the security alarms will all be installed but they can't test them until all the building work is completed. So we must make sure our Tunnel is finished as soon as possible. That bank will then be the mother bank for the region.'

'Charlie, what the fuck is a mother bank?' asked Mick.

'They are holding depot for all the other banks in the region. All the money from all the banks in the south of the country will go to that bank and come from that bank to all the other banks. That's what a holding bank is.'

Billy said, 'That bank could hold more than two hundred bags of spuds.'

'Well, alright,' said Charlie, 'it will be a lot anyway. Right, men, no talking about the bank as Celine is on the way up to the bar.'

'We have to get some women tonight,' said Billy to Mick.

*

Back in the Tunnel the next morning Billy, Charlie and Mick were working as fast as they could to get to the steel rod where the box was. They worked non-stop for four hours digging out the clay and stones that came with it. Charlie turned to Billy, 'Did you calibrate that laser this morning?'

'I calibrate that laser every morning to make sure it's not off line.'

Mick said, 'The shovel is after sliding on the bar.'

'We have it,' said Mick, 'we have it.'

'Stand back,' said Charlie, 'and let the dog see the rabbit.'

While shining the light Billy said, 'The laser spot is shining right on the bar just like we said it would.'

'No,' said Mick, 'just like Charlie said it would shine on the bar. Right, let's dig out the last of the rubble and get it into the wagon and out of here.'

The three men worked clearing out the last of the Tunnel rubble and hauled it up the heist and disposed of it. When it was all cleaned out the box with no bottom, it was removed, and all you could see was a perfect square of solid concrete with a solid three-inch top which was the vault floor nine feet above them. All they have to do now was tidy up and put the hydraulic jack in place to pump the concrete square out.

Charlie said, 'I have a square steel plate less than three foot squared, that has an attachment that will fit onto the hydraulic jack. This square will even the pressure and whole 3 ft^2. It will pop out like a piece of jigsaw. We will get everything in place tonight then we will close down the Tunnel and leave the equipment we are using inside the Tunnel. Every day we must check to see that things are okay.'

The three boys congratulated each other for a job so expertly done.

'All we have to do now is wait and hope that the bank will be up and running for Christmas. Christmas is six weeks away,' Charlie said.

'Billy, we have plenty time now to get ready for this.'

*

The three boys sat in the Tunnel to have a talk. 'We have two tanks,' said Charlie.

'Are we going to fill the two tanks?' asked Mick.

'No,' said Charlie, 'only one that will be enough, the other tank is for all the money sacks and labels from the money which will take some time to remove and transport to the second tank and drop them in.'

'Why is that Charlie?' asked Billy. 'All in good time, Billy, all in good time. And also all the tools that we stole from O'Brien's builders yard will be left here in the Tunnel to be found. So what we must do is fill one of the little rail bins with water and pour in five bottles of thick bleach to wash all our tools and kill the DNA we leave behind. Also, we fill a garden weed sprayer with bleach and spray every piece and every acro in this Tunnel. We then spray the derelict building with the bleach and from that day on when we visit here, we must wear disposable boiler suits to make sure we leave no more fresh DNA. So we will spend the next couple weeks tidying up this building site and preparing for the Christmas raid on the vault.'

'Is the one tank big enough for the money?' said Mick.

'You must remember Mick the most common notes in circulation now are fifties and hundreds, so that means ten of those notes are a grand. You would fit one million in a box the size of a large shoebox, and the bigger notes take less. That tank is big enough when we emptied the bundles in and take off all the wrappers they will sink down and find its own level filling from the ground to the ceiling of that tank. Now remember boys, a lot of cunts out there will be looking for us to take our money so what the three golden words are: silence, silence and more silence. Also, we must not act any different than we have been, and slowly you both fade away from this town. The rats will be out in force looking for us, the drug dealing informers will have a licence to deal if they commit to finding us for the law. So let's finish up now, boys. Come back tomorrow and tidy up some more and secure building site.'

Chapter 15

Charlie, Billy and Mick went to McCarthy's pub later that night, and Celine joined them with two of her friends. Billy and Mick were excited thinking they were getting a woman each.

Charlie said to Billy and Mick, 'If ye play your cards right with them two birds ye will pull them.' So Billy and Mick were on their best behaviour and treating the girls like ladies as that is what they were. They all went back to Charlie's house that night for a late drink and a celebration that the girls didn't know about. Eventually Charlie and Celine went to bed madly in love like always. In the bedroom, Celine played some soft music, she looked at Charlie with the most provocative sexy smile rubbing her own body as she removed her clothes slowly.

'Come and get me, Charlie, if you would like to eat me. Am I your most favourite dessert, Charlie?'

'Yes, you are, my beautiful woman.'

Billy and Mick pulled the two girls but do you know the rules about the girls that don't? This is how it goes. I like the girls that do. I like the girls that don't. I hate the girls that say they will and then you find they won't but the girl I love most of all, each and every night, is the girl that says she doesn't with a smile that says she might. But these are two girls that had a smile that said they might, another night.

The following night after Charlie, Billy and Mick did their inspections in the Tunnel, they all met with the girls: Celine and her friends in McCarthy's pub again, and this time it looked like the boys had pulled it off with the girls because the girls were all over them like a rash.

Charlie was sitting quietly with Celine when suddenly Celine whispered in his ear, 'Do you know the blonde tart that comes in here?'

Charlie replied, 'Blonde tart – why call her a tart, darling? Yes, I often see her in here few times, what about her?'

Celine said, 'If it is true that you were dancing slow dances upstairs with that tramp, I will break your balls.'

Billy sunk into his chair, as he heard the whisper in Charlie's ear. Charlie's face was red. Charlie was talking his way out of the question. Celine went to the toilet with her two friends and Billy said to Charlie, 'How much trouble are you in?'

'Someone told her something,' said Charlie. 'But that is only gossip. I bet it was the man from the end of the bar that was putting the words in her ear but hopefully he doesn't have any facts. If she knew anything, she would not stay here with me tonight, she will be gone.'

*

'Charlie, by Christmas, you will be able to buy any bird you want,' said Billy.

'But you don't understand I am in love with Celine and that's that and you can't buy her or her family, they have money and lots of it. Her father Joseph is building a house worth in the region for over two million.'

'You really are in love with Celine. I can see it in your face. Losing her is your biggest fear, Charlie.'

'Drop the subject, they are on the way back from the toilet.'

'Everything looks fine with Celine,' said Mick.

'Let's bring the girls for a good Chinese meal and a few bottles of champagne. We can well afford it, we have plenty money left over from that job up the country,' said Charlie.

'You said we have to keep a low profile.'

'I did, Billy, but this one night out we deserve it for all our hard work.'

After the meal, Billy and Mick went back to their house with the two girls and Charlie went home to his house with Celine and played some nice music and opened the bottle of champagne he took home with him. Everything was fine. Celine never mentioned anything about Marilyn, so they went to bed and made passionate love. The next morning, the three of them went to the derelict house and checked everything again as usual. Billy turned and saw the postman deliver a letter in their rusty post-box.

'I wonder what it is,' said Mick.

'Go get that, Billy,' said Charlie, 'and see what it is.'

Billy opened the letter and said, 'It is planning permission for this place.'

'For what?' said Mick, laughing. 'To build the Tunnel.'

'No, Mick. Your solicitor applied for planning permission to build two shops here. Did you notice anything about the acros?' asked Charlie.

Nobody replied. 'Look, O'Brien's name is on every one of them. He will not miss them until the day comes when the police will return them to him, asking hundreds of questions. That bastard has robbed the good people of this town for long enough. Must start sending Fred the head a few quid every week. I have to tell you something. O'Brien the builder is going to prison for robbing this bank and building the Tunnel we are standing in.'

Charlie took out the business card he stole from O'Brien's office the day he went there with the hammer in the briefcase. Charlie carefully placed the business card with O'Brien's fingerprints on it under a stone where the police will find it. 'I will go and visit Fred the head this week to renew my friendship with him. And when O'Brien gets arrested for this bank job and remanded in custody, I will then go to Fred the head again and tell him O'Brien killed Celine's cat.'

'Would he care about that?' asked Mick.

'Well, word has it in the prison. If you go near Fred the head's cats at the boiler house, you will go missing up the fucking chimney. Those two prisoners that escaped a few years ago – they did all right. They went up the fucking chimney. One of the guys that went missing only threw a little stone and hit the cat on the head. Fred the head saw him. It did not take long for that guy to go missing. Thirty years, Fred, the head, is in that boiler house shovelling turf into the furnace. He eats, sleeps and drinks in the boiler house. He has thirty cats which he spends any money he gets on, little bells and ribbons for those cats which are his family. When I met Fred in there,' said Charlie, 'I told him I loved cats and instantly Fred was my best friend.'

'How do you think of that one, Charlie?' asked Mick.

'I didn't. It's true, I do love cats.'

'And I love floozy women,' said Billy.

'He said, "If you love cats, you're a good man and you're my friend, and if you ever need a favour just come and ask me".'

A big rock fell out of the wall of the Tunnel and landed on Mick's toe. 'Come on, Mick, let's get you out of here.'

'My toe is broke, Charlie, I can't feel it.'

'You will be okay. Me and Billy will do the Tunnel inspections from now on. We will get you to the hospital.'

*

Mick had to take it easy for a few days because he did have a fractured toe. Charlie and Billy continued to inspect the Tunnel every morning. Everything was in place waiting for the bank to open in a couple of weeks. Charlie, Billy and Mick were enjoying themselves, but every time they got the chance they went over things.

Mick said, 'Tell us more about Fred the head, Charlie. We did not meet him at all.'

'Yes, he is in prison the last thirty years for killing some bloke.'

'So you said that you're going to tell him that O'Brien killed Celine's cat. Will that be a problem for O'Brien?' asked Billy.

'Fucking sure it will.'

'Fuck,' said Mick, 'Fred the head will put O'Brien in the fucking furnace, and the television will say O'Brien escaped just like the rest of them. And O'Brien will never be found either.'

Chapter 16

Charlie and Billy were checking the Tunnel every morning as usual and went for breakfast. They pulled up at the post office to send some money to the cat lover, Fred the head.

'I was dreaming the other night about that boiler house,' said Billy. 'And Fred with all his cats.'

'Did you ever kill a cat?' asked Charlie.

'If I did, Charlie, I would keep that secret to my grave. One never knows when you could be on boiler duty with Fred the head and escape up the fucking chimney in fucking smoke.'

Mick had gone home for a few days as his toe was sore. Charlie and Billy were taking it easy. They were going over the robbery procedure in detail. 'We will use the largest Mercedes van to pack the money into it. We will load it at the back of the derelict house. We will service the van fully and put in a new battery. That will lessen the chances of a breakdown on the night of the job. Make sure it's full of diesel 'cause it has to go way up the country to be scrapped after the job. There is a laneway that goes out to a different street so we can leave the derelict house without anybody seeing the van.'

Driving by the bank they saw all the new office furniture and equipment being unloaded from a truck and carried into the bank. 'It won't be long now,' said Billy, 'it's only two weeks to Christmas. We must now keep an eye on this every day.'

Charlie was spending as much time as he could with Celine so that she will have no suspicion of him. The digging on the Tunnel had been for a few months now and nobody would know when it was exactly dug. By Charlie spending all his time with Celine, she was now his alibi.

The Tunnel was ready for the raid. The hydraulic jack with the three-foot steel plate attached to the top of the extension and going to the floor with a four-inch steel pipe with two ft. square plate on the bottom to stop it sinking into the ground was now in place and ready to be pumped just waiting for Christmas Eve. All the clothing, boots, gloves and hats used for working in the Tunnel were all disposed of. All the tools were washed with bleach but left in the Tunnel because they belonged to O'Brien the builders. Charlie's house and the house where Billy and Mick stayed were all washed and cleaned. Charlie had bought new boiler suits, ski masks, boots and gloves for the raid which would take place on Christmas Eve.

Chapter 17

Charlie collected the kids and took them over the mountains to the monks' abbey. The kids brought their jars of money that they collected since the last time they visited it. When the kids were fighting to put the money in the slots, Charlie said a few prayers. Charlie looked up at the ceiling at a big painting of our Lord looking down with his arms open wide. Charlie said, 'I always kept the pennies for you, God, and I will be able to put a lot more in the slots for you very soon. They will be able to rebuild the old leaking roof. And paint the whole Abbey. In St Antony's Chapel the bells will ring again because they will have the money to repair them. I also guarantee you God, O'Brien the builders will not be up here doing the job and robbing your monks.'

Just as Charlie left the Abbey with the kids he looked back and up at the ceiling again and said, 'It's all up to you now, God.' When he turned to leave a monk was standing in front of him. Charlie was startled because the monk was so close to him.

The monk said, 'Hello. I see you come here from time to time with the kids and give us some money. Thank you very much.'

'That's okay,' said Charlie.

The monk was very old and held Charlie by the hand and said, 'Shall we go for a little walk up and down the avenue while the kids play around the grounds?'

'Okay,' said Charlie.

'I won't keep you very long,' said the monk. 'My name is Father John O'Brien. What is yours?'

'My name is Charles Anthony Green.' Walking down the driveway the monk got into conversation with Charlie about life in general. On the way back up, Father John asked, 'How long is it, Charlie, since your last confession?'

'It's about 20 years.'

'Well, that is a long time, Charlie, and you do know that you can make a confession at any time in any place? So as we walk you can start.'

'Okay, Father – where do I start?'

'Well, you can start with "bless me Father for I have sinned".'

'Okay, Father. Bless me Father for I have sinned. It's 20 years since my last confession. So I now ask you Lord for forgiveness for what I have done, and what I have failed to do and all the other sins I'd like you to take into consideration.'

'Kneel down, Charlie.' When Charlie knelt down on the gravel driveway to say an act of contrition Father John said as he blessed Charlie:

"Ego te absolvo a peccatis tuis in nomine Patris et filii et spiritus sancti."

"Oh my God, I'm sorry for having offended thee and with your help I will not sin again. I bless you, Charlie, in the name of the Father and of the son and of the Holy Spirit, amen."

The bells of St. Mary's Chapel started ringing at same time as the absolution prayer. The kids were looking out of the jeep, laughing at Daddy on his knees praying.

Chapter 18

The bank was now open and running for a few weeks. They were getting ready for tomorrow night as it was Christmas Eve. Charlie, Billy and Mick were going over the last of the plan. 'We must take all clothing to the derelict house where we will change before we do the job. Listen men,' said Charlie. 'I expect the alarm to activate the minute we penetrate the floor of the vault with the hydraulic jack. So once the floor breaks open, we must act fast. We must remove the concrete and a hydraulic jack out of the Tunnel, and we have a ladder ready to go up into the vault. When we enter the vault, I will secure the door with the pulley block chain that will go back down the Tunnel and out to the derelict building by a steel rope attached to the chain at the other end of the steel rope, where the pulley chain will be attached. When this is tightened up to its full pressure, it will have five tonnes pulling power keeping the door of the vault pulling it closed.

'Billy and Mick – you must bring in the stepladder and secure the curtain to the ceiling of the vault one foot away from the walls. This will take us about 15 minutes. Once we have the chain on the door they can't get in even if they override the timers and the locks which I don't expect them to.'

'Charlie, you know how it works because you did work for security alarm companies some years ago.'

'Part of my job,' said Charlie, 'was to try and bypass the alarm system. Sometimes I did and sometimes I didn't. It all depends on how much money you are willing to spend on the system. So you must be sure that the bank has the best system. The only chance we have of a poor system in that bank is that O'Brien cut corners and got a cheap system. The bank will set the alarm tomorrow at closing time. The vault time locks will be set not to open for the Christmas holiday, for five days.'

'How will we move out the bags of money?' asked Mick

'The spuds,' said Charlie.

'Yes,' said Mick, 'the spuds.'

Billy was walking around impatient for Charlie to answer Mick. 'We will draw the money down the Tunnel loaded on to the two rail carriages we have, and push it to the end of the Tunnel, empty the carriages and come back until we have the amount we want in the basement of the derelict house. Then Mick will be upstairs on the ground floor, and we throw the bags up one by one. Then the three of us will then take them out the back of the derelict house and load them into the van with as much as we can fit in.'

'Will Celine be wondering where we are on Christmas Eve?'

'Well, what we do is hit the bank minutes after they close, that way all the staff would be committed to parties and family and nearly impossible to locate when the alarm activates.'

'What are you buying Celine for a Christmas present?' asked Mick.

'That is a secret. Show ye tomorrow night when I give it to her.'

*

'We have everything ready for tomorrow night. I have the black curtain ready with the nylon cord to hang it already in place, and all you have to do Billy is use the Hilti nail gun to put the four anchors in each corner of the vault and loop on the curtain to the bars that come out one foot from the wall. This gives us a one-foot perimeter of darkness.'

'What is the curtain for?' asked Mick.

'All in good time, Mick, all in good time. Now I must tell ye men what a wise man once told me. Very clever, intelligent people have carried out very clever, intelligent jobs in intelligent ways. They did the job with expertise, they got the money and or the gold, but he said to me that the only part of the job they all forgot to plan properly is what happens after. Some fuck up because the money goes to their brain. They go on to drink, and some go on the drugs, and also, they hunt for women. Now this speech is not just for you two. It's for me as well. I'm just human like ye are. What we must do is not do what all the other wise men did after the clever jobs. We will not spend money buying gifts for anybody. We will not carry cash in our wallets, just enough for a few drinks. We will not buy clothes or fast cars or slow ones for that matter. You may be sure when we are in McCarthy's pub or nightclub all the babes will be on the hunt for the smell of money. So if they see you buying drink, splashing cash, we will be tumbled. The plan to rob the bank is now completed. The plan to prevent us getting caught for robbing that bank is only beginning.'

'We have a lot of money to think about,' said Mick.

'I know,' said Charlie. 'I have that planned out in my head. To get past the ring of steel. You know I did my pilots licence last summer for a small plane? I will fly the money in small amounts like a few million to the exchange man that will move it out of the country. I will explain more about that when the time is right. Because it's winter I will have to wait just a few weeks for good weather in the early spring to fly it out and fly back on the same night. I changed my car a few months ago so that nobody would be sniffing around at it, because they see I had it before the job. When we go to McCarthy's nightclub you will feel the magnetic field in that place trying to hone in on anybody that knew anything about the robbery. So we must be exactly the same as we were before. I don't expect anything to come our direction because the police will go a different direction, following the tracks and clues I deliberately left for them. Every time I say to you both all in good time, all in good time. Each one of those is a clue for the brilliance of a good detective investigator who is worth his salt. I will say no more about that for now. Only this. All in good time, all in good time.

'So this is the end of my speech on Christmas Eve. Tomorrow night we will be rich men. But we must remember we will be the most wanted men this country has ever seen. They don't give a fuck what crimes you commit as much as they give a fuck about robbing one of their national banks. Take it from me they are coming after the ones that robbed this bank so now my loyal and trusted comrades, we must finish this debate on the job. Have you any questions for me before we adjourn this meeting?'

'Okay, we all meet in McCarthy's pub between nine and ten tonight.'

Charlie then left and went to Celine's father's new house. Celine was there showing her father the way he should arrange the furniture. Joseph lived on his own since Celine's mother died and built the new house to accommodate all the in laws and grandchildren. Celine grew up not knowing what it was like to have no money. She was lucky in that way. Some girls that need to have money can train themselves to love any type of man that is able to provide it.

The doorbell rang and Joseph answered the door. 'Hello, Charlie.'

'Hello, Joseph, has Celine called round, she said she'd meet here?'

'Yes, she is somewhere around the house, probably in the kitchen.'

'This house is fabulous, Joseph.'

'Well, if not for you O'Brien the builder would have got away with a shoddy job. So thank you for what you did to make him sort it out.'

'Will you have a drink, Charlie?'

'No, Joseph, I won't, you know me I park up the jeep before I go drinking.'

'That's good, Charlie, you never know when someone could walk out in front of you.'

Celine walked into the room, 'Hello, my darling,' she said with that beautiful provocative smile. 'I love you, my handsome man.'

'And I love you, my beautiful young woman.' This was the first time he sensed the fear looking at Celine. *What if the bank job went wrong and how could I live with myself in prison away from Celine for years*? This would be the worst possible thing that could happen to Charlie right now. *I love this woman more than all the money in the world, never mind the holding bank.*

'Are you joining us in McCarthy's tonight? Mick and Billy will be there? Bring your friends and we will have a good time.'

'I hope that Marilyn one won't be stalking my man tonight.'

'Her name is Jane Eastwood and let's not talk about her, darling.'

'She's not going to give up till she gets her claws into you – that slapper.'

'Okay, darling, leave it at that.'

'I will see you in McCarthy's before nine, and I will bring my two girlfriends for Billy and Mick.'

Chapter 19

By the time nine o'clock came around they were all in McCarthy's having a good time. Joseph was there in his new suit looking the business. Celine and two friends were there in the arms of Mick and Billy.

Charlie whispered into Celine's ear, 'Will you marry me?' With the music so loud Celine had to ask Charlie to repeat what he said even though she did catch the words but wanted to hear them again just to be sure. 'Will you marry me, Celine, because I love you more than anything in this world, and I never want to lose you?'

Celine was smiling with delight and said, 'Of course, I will marry you, I love you too.'

Charlie put his hand into his pocket and took out a piece of brown paper and handed it to Celine. She opened it slowly and she found the most beautiful engagement ring inside. Everybody now in the company had realised what just went down.

Billy shouted, 'You asked Celine to marry you, and you gave her the engagement ring, but we didn't hear you ask, so will you please say that again for our ears. Barman, turn down the music for one minute.'

When the music was lowered Charlie turned to Celine again and said, 'They needed to hear it – will you please marry me?'

Celine replied, 'I'd be delighted to.'

Then Joseph ordered two bottles of champagne, and everybody had a toast to Charlie and Celine and their happiness together. Celine turned around and said out loud, 'Will we be married before the next eight months because I'd like to tell my fiancé I'm having his baby. I am one month pregnant.' Joseph turned round to the barman shocked at what his daughter said. 'Barman, give me a large brandy before I faint with the shock that I'm going to be a grandad again.'

Celine continued, 'Well, if it is before the eighth month and after the sixth month, I will need a large dress. If it's before third month, I will need small dress.'

Charlie turned to Celine and said, 'All that is now in your hands, you tell me where and when, and I will be there.'

*

Celine put her arms around Charlie and whispered in his ear, 'Are you happy that you are now going to be a daddy again?'

'Of course, I am, darling. I am delighted and excited. I love you so much.'

'Now let me tell you, my darling,' said Celine, 'your galavanting days are over. As from after Christmas, wherever you go so do I.'

'Okay, darling, I know.'

'I have to accept my responsibilities now. I will choose to get married in four weeks' time so that I won't be showing my pregnancy too much. This way we will be man and wife when our baby is born and that is the way it should be.'

'I know,' said Charlie, 'it is very important to you Jewish people to be married before you have a baby and you will be.'

Billy and Mick were engrossed in conversation with Celine's two friends. They had been together before but now they seemed to be hitting it off big time. Joseph had gone home; he had an earlier night than he expected because of the shock of his daughter's announcement of a wedding, and the baby got him drunk.

The three girls went to the toilet. Billy said, 'What time are we making a start tomorrow, Charlie?'

'I'd say we should be ready at two o'clock in the afternoon.'

'Okay, we can have a sleep in in the morning.'

'So you're going to be a daddy again, Charlie?' said Mick.

'Yes, I am, and I'm over the moon.'

'You know you won't be philandering after Christmas. That's over, you will be under the thumb.'

Billy said, 'Here are the three girls back, and Marilyn just made an exit out the side door. I bet they said something to her in the toilet.'

Celine said, when she sat on her seat after returning from the toilet, 'I just fixed that blonde slapper that had her eye on my man. It was too good of an opportunity. I stuck the ring in her face and said, "Charlie just asked me to marry him and also I'm having his baby in the New Year after we get married. So now, run along dear." You wouldn't get a better arena than that toilet here in McCarthy's to slice that tramp out of our lives. She is a dumb fucking blonde. God bless her,' said Celine, 'if you shot her point blank in the head, she would live.'

Charlie said nothing only nodded his head hoping the subject would go away. This secret of him with Marilyn was haunting his brain.

Billy said, 'Let's go upstairs with the girls and have a good time.'

*

Christmas Eve – Morning.

Charlie got out of bed, it was noon. He had a good sleep after a good night out. Celine had left earlier this morning. The doorbell rang, it was Billy and Mick.

'Let's have a cup of coffee,' said Charlie. 'We will go over the final plan now. Everything we need is in the derelict house, all we have to do is collect the van and drive it down the back lane and into the yard of the derelict building. Is there anything you have to say, men, because now is the time?

Charlie dropped off Billy and Mick to where the van was parked.

'Is the van full with diesel?'

'Yes,' Billy said.

'Did you put a new battery in it?'

'Yes.'

'Okay, see you around the corner from the back lane where I will park up my jeep.'

Charlie hopped into the van after he parked up the jeep not far from the back lane. Billy drove around to the back-gate entrance, Mick got out, and opened the corrugated ten-foot gate. They drove in. Mick closed the gate. As they drove down the lane Charlie said. 'Mick, I forgot to thank you for getting the digger and tidying up the lane a few weeks ago.'

'That's all right, we are just doing our bit. It's now two o'clock in the afternoon and that bank is going to close for the Christmas at three o'clock. Once they close the vault the time locks will be set for four days.' The boys entered the derelict house and put on their boiler suits, gloves and boots and ski masks. They entered the Tunnel and made ready the two hundred tonne hydraulic jack in position and jacked it touching the floor. They secured the five tonne pulley blocks in the derelict house and had a steel rope coming up the Tunnel and on the end of that, they had a chain with a hook on it ready. They had the black curtain and nylon cord on. They had four anchors that they were going to put on the ceiling wall with a Hilti gun.

'As soon as we break through the floor we work fast. We don't want them to come back to the bank and open the vault if they could. It's ten to three now. Billy – you can see the bank front door from the top floor. So when we break through you go up to the top floor and see what activities are outside the bank. We will hit the vault the minute the staff leaves for the Christmas holiday. Go now Billy and see them coming out.'

Billy went to the top floor and just as he got there, he saw the last of the staff coming out the door. The manager was switching on the alarms and turning the keys in the two locks on the door. Billy came running down the stairs and into the Tunnel and said, 'This is it. They are all gone, the bank is now closed for the whole Christmas period.'

'Right lads, let's get to work. Start pumping the hydraulic jack.' On the jack gauge they could see eight tonnes of pressure on the dial. Billy said, 'It is not going to go, Charlie.'

'It will, Billy. Keep pumping there, Mick.'

Mick pumped and pumped and the pressure went up to one hundred tonnes of pressure. 'That's hard concrete,' said Billy.

Then there was a snap sound coming from the floor, the pressure dropped on the jack to ten tonnes. 'It's gone,' said Charlie. 'Keep jacking and Billy take over the pump.'

Billy pumped and pumped and Jack rose with the slab of the concrete on it. The concrete slab was now six inches up into the floor; they released the pressure and the jack returned down into the hole. Mick and Billy lifted the end of the jack out of the hole. Billy dragged it out of the Tunnel. Mick and Charlie were lifting out the slab of concrete by turning it sideways down into the hole. They put it on the ground and lifted the ladder into place. Charlie went up the ladder and Mick pulled up the big curtain and the tools. Charlie needed the end of the chain and then Billy and Mick entered the hole into the vault. Charlie opened up the plate on the vault door and hooked the chain onto the bar inside the door plate.

'It's ready.'

Billy ran down the ladder and out to the pulley blocks at the derelict house and took up the slack on the chain slowly, the pressure came on as Billy ratcheted the pulley blocks, five tonne pressure so now the door could not be opened. Billy went to the top floor of the derelict house and looked out the window and saw the alarm was now activated.

It was expected that the alarm would be activated as soon as the floor snapped open. Billy ran down into the Tunnel and into the vault and helped put up the black curtain. The men hung the curtain one foot away from every wall in the vault.

Billy said, 'The alarm is ringing,' but they could not hear it in the vault. Each man had on a miner's light on his head. In the vault there were shelving racks all around and they were full of bags of cash the sacks with heavy plastic so you could see the size of the notes inside.

'What will happen now?' said Billy.

'The cops will ring the bank manager and tell him the security alarm has been activated in the bank. He's only gone home twenty minutes and automatically he will think it's a false alarm because it's so soon after closing. It doesn't matter anyway, they can't get in here even if they override the locks. So let's get to work, pick out the largest notes first, Billy. You go down the hole and fill the wagon bins as we throw them down. Do not clog up the Tunnel. Get the bags out into the basement. We can move them from there once we have them out of the vault and out of the Tunnel.'

'There must be three hundred bags here, Charlie,' said Mick.

'Doesn't matter, Mick. We just take as many as we can.' Billy was loading the miniature railway wagons which took about ten sacks each in large notes. Billy emptied the wagons in the basement and returned up the Tunnel to find Charlie and Mick had dumped down ten more. Mick came down the ladder to help Billy transport the sacks to the wagons. Then Billy said, 'I will go to the top floor to see if the manager has come to turn off the alarm.'

The manager of the bank got the phone call from the alarm company and the police went to the bank when the alarm was activated.

'Okay, Detective Sweeney, I will be in the bank in ten minutes,' said the manager. At the bank Detective Rice and Detective Sweeney were waiting outside. The manager opened the door and the three entered. The manager was saying it must be a false alarm as we were only closed thirty-five minutes ago.

'What are you going to do about the alarm for the Christmas if it keeps activating?' asked Detective Sweeney.

'I will try reset the alarm for now, and it should be alright.'

'Okay,' said Detective Sweeney. The manager went to the alarm panel and entered the code and reset the alarm and the bells and sirens went silent. 'It's reset now.'

As they left the bank the two policemen said, 'Happy Christmas, Mr Reilly.'

The bank manager said, 'And a happy New Year to the two of you as well.'

The manager locked the bank door and they all went about their business. Back in the vault, now that the alarm was silent they could work away without interruption. Billy was back watching from the top floor when the cops and the bank manager were going in to check the alarm out. When he saw them leave, he returned to the vault. 'They're gone,' Billy said. 'The two cops and the manager entered the bank and silenced the alarm or reset it.'

*

Mick said, 'Have you seen the labels on the sacks? Some of them say one million others are five hundred thousand.'

'How much is there?' enquired Billy.

'Fucking millions,' said Mick. 'Charlie was right, it is fucking huge.' Billy and Mick went up the ladder back into the vault and said to Charlie, 'We must have two hundred bags out there, and there is one million in some of them.'

'I notice that,' said Charlie, 'and look what I found.' Charlie opened a fancy wooden box and showed the boys five thousand gold coins. 'Now boys this box is not for us. This box is going to charity so forget that you ever saw it. Because it's easier for me to give the religious people this box of gold rather than cash. It's probably worth half a million or more, I don't know. But I'm giving it to them, anyway.'

'No problem, Charlie,' said Billy.

'Give them more if you want,' said Mick.

'Do you think what we have in the basement will fill the van?'

'It probably could,' said Billy.

'No,' Mick said. 'I reckon only three quarters, keep throwing out the bags. Some of the bags are the size of a double shoebox, others are bigger. All the small bags are gone out it's only big bags left, the floor underneath, and the shelves are stacked with coins. We're not taken the fucking coins are we?' said Billy.

'No, we're not,' said Charlie.

'Well, let's get out and fill the van, it is now dark outside. We must get this job over by nine o'clock and then nobody will be wondering where we are. We get back to the pub to be seen in public.'

Celine was out doing her last Christmas shopping. It was difficult for her to find something really special for Charlie to wear over the Christmas, but she'd think she had got a beautiful Italian suit. Her father Joseph had given her ten grand for Christmas and she was so happy looking forward to the New Year getting married and having a new baby.

O'Brien the builder was in his office collecting his last cheque that the bank sent him for the building. He was very pleased with himself for robbing the bank manager out of thousands on extra charges. 'Christmas is good,' said O'Brien putting the cheque in his pocket and saying it's not often I get to rob a bank. The secretary in the office despised O'Brien because he was so mean and slobbered in her face as if he had a chance with her. He said to his office girl that he might just fuck off after Christmas and have a good time for a few weeks, expecting an answer from the girl who was pretending she was not listening to his dull humour.

Charlie asked Celine to buy some presents for each of his two children he had in another relationship. She got them some presents and Christmas cards and put some cash in each card, a few hundred each.

Chapter 20

Charlie, Billy and Mick left the vault. Charlie and Billy stayed down in the basement. Mick went up to the ground floor. One by one Charlie and Billy threw the bags up to Mick. Mick stacked them in the hallway of the derelict house until all the bags were all up. Then the three boys carried the bags out the back and loaded them into the Mercedes van neatly.

Billy said to Charlie, 'Will the contents of the van fit down into the tank? Is the tank big enough to hold all the money?'

'It is, Billy.'

'You must remember ye are removing all the bags and wrappers from the money so it will find its own level when ye dump it down into the tank. It will fill every crevice of the tank as it piles up. You will be surprised how much will fit into that tank.'

They pushed the door closed against the money in the van. Charlie walked up the lane and opened the lock on the gate and returned to the van. Billy and Mick were changing their clothes just inside the door of the derelict house. 'There are your clothes over there, Charlie.'

When all the clothes were changed, all the working clothes were put into black bin bag and went with the van. Charlie said, 'You know the drill. Take them clothes and burn them at the old bonfire site. When you get to the tank take out the bags one by one. Then take all the wrappers and all the money bands and put them into the large sack at the tank. Then when you have all the money loaded down into the tank, bring all the old bags and money wrappers to the second tank and put them all in and then dispose of the sack you carried them in to make it look like that is where we had the money for a while. I will do the last bleach spray in the vault and the Tunnel and around the house before I leave. Go now.'

Billy started the van and drove down the back lane to the gate. Charlie opened the gate and looked to see if the coast was clear. He gave the nod and the boys drove out and away without stopping. Charlie returned to the house and got the weed sprayer and started spraying bleach everywhere. He went into the vault and sprayed everywhere. When everything was sprayed right up to the back door he left and pushed in the back door closed. It was now eight o'clock, and Charlie was leaving with a big holdall with the sprayer inside it.

It was a freezing cold dark night as Charlie was walking down the road to his silver jeep he had parked. As he went around the corner, he saw a dozen men standing outside the YMCA waiting to go in. Charlie had on his hoody over his baseball cap and a scarf around his face when he saw the men standing in the freezing cold waiting to go in for a bed for the night. The door would be open soon to let the men in. Charlie got a guilty feeling in his bones. He quickly returned to the laneway, opened the back gate, went in and closed it behind him. He went in the back door of the derelict building, down the ladder to the basement, emptied out the sprayer from the holdall, took out his pocket torch and entered the Tunnel up the ladder into the vault. He filled the holdall with cash and zipped it up and left. He quickly exited the lane and closed the gate. Just as he got to the YMCA the door was opening. He could hear the men in the queue saying to each other how cold it was. The YMCA man said, 'Off to bed now, lads, no messing around here tonight. It is Christmas Eve so I want no trouble from any of ye tonight.'

The bulbs in the YMCA were the lowest watt and cheapest on the market to save electricity. A little more than a candle. Charlie followed the queue upstairs to a dormitory and picked out one of the beds that you could barely see with the one candle watt bulb. All the men quickly got into bed complaining about the cold, and mostly talking to themselves. The YMCA man came into the room. Charlie was in bed with the holdall under the bed. 'Lights out now, lads.' He turned off the light.

You could only see around the room with the light coming in the window from the street lights. Charlie was in bed with his clothes on just like all the men in the room. Charlie got out of bed, picked up the holdall, unzipped the bag and went around to each bed with a bundle of money half the size of a shoebox for each man. He said as he went to each bed, 'Happy Christmas' and handed a bundle. The men were all talking to themselves.

One said, 'My God, I now believe in Santa again.'

'So do I,' said another.

'It must be an angel from God has come to us tonight to make our Christmas. God bless you whoever you are,' said a voice in the corner.

Charlie turned around and said, 'I'm about to leave now, men. All I ask is you keep away from the cops and tell nobody about your Christmas presents. Happy Christmas, I'm off now.'

*

Charlie quickly left the YMCA and walked to his jeep and drove home to get ready as they were all meeting in McCarthy's between nine and ten o'clock. Charlie thought to himself while driving home, how pitiful it was to see those men in the YMCA freezing with the cold and nothing for Christmas. He thought that some of those men were highly educated but for one's circumstances are another. Things just went wrong for them. Either through drug addiction, or alcoholism, sometimes it's not by choice, it is a genetic addiction that they were born with which they had no control over. But hopefully the money he gave them would bring them a happy Christmas. Maybe one or two of them will have enough to get back up from where they are.

Back at the YMCA, the men were whispering to each other. One went out the hallway to check if the caretaker was around, but there was no sign of him. They turned on the light and had a look at how much money they each had. One of them turned around and said, 'I think I have hundred grand.' And he could hear his friends say, 'And so do I, and me too.'

So they all gathered around one bed when they had their money put away in their bag under the bed. 'We must leave early in the morning for the city, it's Christmas day, but there is still one train to the city at 9 am. If we get it, we can get new clothing as some shops never close. Then we can book into a hotel for a few days and have a proper Christmas dinner. Who's in favour?'

They all put their hands up. So the next morning all the men booked out of the YMCA. Before the caretaker had done his rounds, they were all at the railway station waiting to board the train to the city. Never would you see more happy faces than the faces of these men waiting to board that train to the city.

*

Charlie drove home, had a shower and put all the clothes he was wearing in another bag and the put them into his woodburning stove which was lighting since this morning. He piled in some logs to make sure there were no traces of them. It was nearly nine o'clock when he walked in the door of McCarthy's pub; Billy and Mick were standing at the bar. Celine, her two sisters and father where in the pub in deep conversation. Charlie tried to blend in as if he was there earlier.

Billy said to Charlie, 'Everything went like clockwork. Everything is done – the diesel tank is full, we had to push the money down to get it to close.'

'Did you put the sacks and money labels in the other tank?'

'Yes,' said Billy. 'We did exactly what you told us to.'

'Where is the Mercedes van?'

'In a day or two we will take it up north and have it scrapped.'

'Okay, boys – this is where we must not make the mistakes. We have done the job and we've got away with the job. We must not slip up now and get caught for it. But for now, it's Christmas Eve. Happy Christmas, Billy, and Happy Christmas, Mick.'

'Happy Christmas, Charlie.'

*

Charlie got Celine's attention and beckoned her to come closer to him.

'Hi, my darling,' said Celine.

Charlie said into Celine's ear, 'Have you thought about the wedding?'

'Yes, my darling,' she replied.

'I think we should go for the beginning of February, if that's all right with you.'

'That's fine, so we say the first weekend in February,' said Charlie. 'I will now leave it in your hands to plan everything.'

'Okay, my darling and another thing – Daddy is paying for everything.'

'I can well afford to pay for our wedding. But I will leave your father to pay for it or he might get uptight about it if I don't allow him to.'

'Yes, my darling, don't prevent my daddy from paying. That makes Daddy very proud.'

'So, Celine, this is your wedding and you must see that it's all done your way. It's not a man's thing to plan the wedding, because Celine, darling, I would not know where to start.' Charlie thought this will keep Celine busy while he's sorting out the money in their hideout. 'My darling, tomorrow is Christmas Day and before Christmas dinner I must go and see an old friend in the monks' abbey over the mountains.'

'Okay, my darling. Charlie, we are having Christmas dinner in my father's house, everything will be ready at two o'clock. Because it's Christmas Eve, McCarthy's will be closed by midnight and everybody will be retiring home to their houses for Christmas Day.'

Celine put her arms around Charlie and said, 'Happy Christmas, my darling,' and kissed him on the lips.

Charlie replied, 'I love you and happy Christmas.'

Charlie had got some lovely presents delivered to Joseph's house. Presents for Celine and all her family. Celine was out shopping and got Charlie some lovely new clothes. Billy and Mick stood up with everybody and said, 'We will see you all after Christmas. We must go home to the city to our families.' They didn't drink any alcohol as they were to take it in turns to drive.

Before they left the pub, they had a quick chat with Charlie. Just as Billy was leaving, he said to Charlie, 'I'm a bit short, could you give me a few notes for the petrol?'

Charlie whispered, 'You bad boys are tapping me on Christmas Eve.'

'Don't worry,' said Billy. 'I will pay it back in the New Year.' Charlie took out his wallet and gave Mick and Billy one hundred each and said, 'Happy Christmas – see you in the New Year.'

This was done because he knew people were watching and Celine overheard what they were saying. Charlie was thinking to himself, *How can the bank now pinpoint the time of the robbery so they can't pinpoint the time we were missing and we need an alibi for.*

This would also mean O'Brien could not come up with an alibi that would cover him for the whole week. Charlie was thinking to himself, *I wonder how much we have? Around two hundred million I suppose – a lot of money to be cared for in a very secret way. I would love to bring Celine up to where the money is and do the bold thing in the tank of money under a red bulb. I will have to go down a good few million before we would fit in the tank.*

Charlie's mother arrived home for Christmas two days before and he never knew until Celine told him at McCarthy's. It was a surprise visit for Charlie. Everybody retired back to Joseph's house after the pub closed. After a few drinks, Charlie and Celine went to bed. Joseph was asleep on the couch with a rug over him.

Chapter 21

Charlie got up early Christmas morning and went to see his children from his previous relationship he had prior to meeting Celine. He loaded up his jeep with all the Christmas presents and Christmas cards and drove to the kids' house. It was 9 am and the town was deserted. Charlie gave the kids all the presents and they were excited opening them. Every time they saw a new present they jumped up and hugged their daddy with excitement. They opened their cards and took out all the cash they received from Charlie, Mick, Billy, Joseph and Celine.

    He said to the kids, 'Let's get in the jeep and go visit holy God's house over the mountains.' The kids took some of their toys with them to play with on their trip over the mountains. Charlie often took the kids to the monks Abbey from time to time. The kids always brought some money for the monks that they collected in jars. The kids had a jar of coins each to put in the poor box in St Mary's Chapel. When Charlie arrived at the monastery and parked outside St Mary's Chapel, the kids knew the drill and where to go and went running off. Charlie took out the box from under the seat of the jeep, concealed in a plastic bag. Charlie entered the chapel and went to the confessional box – the part where the priest sat to hear your confession. He opened the confessional and placed the box of gold coins on the seat with a note saying: *"Don't spend God's money foolishly. God also expects a good job done on the roof and the renovations."* He closed the confessional door but was spotted by a monk closing the door of his confessional. Charlie joined the kids lighting a few candles. The kids were kneeling and saying the prayers to God.

Charlie knelt down and looked up at the ceiling and said, 'I kept my promise. I will check progress to see if you need more later in the year.' Charlie blessed himself and beckoned the kids to come along. When he turned to leave, he saw the monk with the box and note in his hand. Obviously, he inspected it and knew what he got. The monk bowed his head to Charlie as he left St Mary's Chapel with the kids holding a hand each. Charlie bowed and continued to exit.

In the jeep on the way back the kids said to Daddy, 'You gave holy God no money this time, Daddy?'

'I gave ye all the money for him.'

'But that was our money, Daddy,' said Ellie May.

'No, Ellie, the money was from all of us,' said Jerome. 'Will holy God love us for giving him money?' asked Jerome.

'Of course, he loves us, Jerome.' Driving out the driveway Charlie thought to himself, *Well, they have at least half one million to start on the roof. I will drop them another million if they need it. I will monitor the progress.* Charlie turned to the kids, 'We must come up to holy God's house more often.'

'Okay, Daddy,' said Ellie Mai.

'Ellie Mai and Jerome – I will collect you later in the afternoon and take you up to Joseph's house.'

Charlie dropped off the kids and headed to Joseph's house for Christmas dinner. Celine and her sisters were preparing a Christmas feast.

Charlie had passed the bank on the way back from the mountains and the alarms were still silent.

*

Charlie walked into Joseph's house. Sitting at the table with Joseph was Charlie's mother Josey. Josey stood up and put her arms around Charlie and said, 'Son, I love you, and have a Happy Christmas. Have a lovely marriage with your fiancée, Celine.'

'Happy Christmas, Mother, and a happy New Year to you too.' For the next two hours the Christmas dinner was a huge affair and huge preparations by Celine and her family. Charlie stood up and made a toast to Joseph, his beautiful new house and to his beautiful daughters for preparing this lovely dinner. 'Happy Christmas to my beautiful fiancée and happy New Year to everybody.'

Everybody was replying, 'Happy New Year,' and toasting glasses.

Later on in the afternoon, Charlie went back and collected Ellie Mai and Jerome as he had promised. Joseph's house had ten bedrooms, en suite. Charlie said to Celine, 'I will go up and have a little sleep. Then I will have a shower and change my clothes before I bring the kids back home.' Just when it was getting dark, Charlie put the kids in the jeep and drove them home. On the way back he diverted to O'Brien the builder's office. He parked the car around the corner and put on his gloves, woolly hat, coat and scarf. He walked around to O'Brien's office quickly. It was in a secluded place where nobody would take notice of you in the back street. He knelt down and picked the front door lock and entered the office.

He took out a piece of paper from his pocket, lifted up the phone and dialled the number. A lady's voice spoke at the other end and said, 'NBC News. Can I help you?'

'Yes, I would like to advise you that a huge story is about to break in Charlestown in the next two days so crews should make their way here immediately.' Charlie hung up the phone and went over to the planning permission drawer and took out the planning map that he put a pin mark on months before. He pinned the map on the map board where a dozen other maps were and then he left the office and picked the door closed. Now the news team would think O'Brien made that call before the news got out of the bank robbery.

Charlie returned to Celine's father's house and had some champagne with the family and his mother. Things couldn't be better. Christmas Day, everything was closed so they spent the whole day and night in Joseph's house celebrating Christmas. Mick and Billy were on the phone from their homes and family having a good Christmas. Nobody mentioned the job to anybody. None of them had spent extra money this Christmas so nobody could gossip about them.

But Charlie thought to himself: *Next year Christmas will be different. We will spend whatever we want.*

Wednesday morning, the bank opened at 9 am for all the business people in the town to lodge the Christmas takings. There was a large crowd queueing at the tellers. Charlie joined the queue to withdraw some money from his account to give to his mother before she returned home. Before Charlie got served at the counter the girl inside said, 'We have run out of coins because we are having trouble opening the vault. So could you come back later?' she said to the customer in the queue next to Charlie's queue. Having heard this, Charlie left the bank. The bank had not discovered the robbery yet, and it would be some time before they would get access to the vault. Customers in the bank were told later that day that the vault door mechanism had malfunctioned, and it would right itself in the next twenty-four hours.

That fifty-tonne chain will keep them out of that vault for longer than twenty-four hours, Charlie thought. It would be days before they gain access because that vault is made to keep people out. Christmas was winding down, but now the New Year will start all the celebrations going again. After the New Year celebrations the town usually turns into a ghost town the first week in January. This year it would be the busiest year ever when the news would break that the bank was robbed. It came out on the radio that the banks in the county were running short of cash because the holding centre vault door had malfunctioned. The bank had reassured the public that the situation would be rectified as soon as possible. Thursday had come and gone; the bank manager called in the expert locksmiths that installed bank vault doors.

Charlie phoned Billy and Mick and said, 'We are going for a drink Friday night as usual. It's a very quiet Christmas down here,' he said to Billy.

'Yes and is a very quiet Christmas up here as well. No money around over the recession.'

'So I will see you both in McCarthy's early Friday night which is New Year's Eve. We celebrate and ring in the New Year in the nightclub.'

'Okay, Charlie, we will see you then.'

Celine was putting the final touches to the New Year's Eve dinner at her father's house before they went to McCarthy's pub. Charlie was in deep thought. *I have really taken a fancy to Joseph's new house, and the day will come when I will ask him to give that house to his daughter for a wedding present and take my word, he will not refuse my offer. I just have to work out what way I will say it to him. It's a ten-bedroom, large dining halls, studies and offices all in one with a swimming pool off the back side. It has a games room with a snooker table and the cinema section at one end.*

*

The security company had worked round-the-clock taking out the whole cheap security system that O'Brien builders cut corners installing. Friday afternoon and the bank had not opened the vault yet. They couldn't understand why the door won't open. NBC News was starting to get suspicious about the story as to why the bank vault door won't open. Detective Rice and Detective Sweeney called to the bank and said to the bank manager, 'What the fuck is going on that you can't override the system and open the door?'

'You have my permission to talk to the security men that are working round-the-clock since Wednesday removing all the security systems that we have on the premises, and when that was done the vault would not open.'

Detective Sweeney said, 'NBC News is making us look like fools. They are now parked across the road showing live footage of the bank.'

Detective Rice said to the bank manager, 'From the way NBC News is talking, they seem to know something. They must have heard something. I smell a rat.'

Detective Sweeney spoke to the security technician, 'What the fuck is going on with this vault door?'

The technician turned around and said, 'I don't know, we are going to drill a pencil-sized hole through the reinforced concrete wall which is three foot thick.'

'How long is this going to take?' asked Detective Sweeney.

The technician said, 'About two hours – you must remember there are reinforced bars in that concrete that are two inches thick.'

The manager was speaking live on NBC News and explained that the technicians were drilling a pencil-sized hole in the vault wall to put in a fish lens camera and see what is going on inside.

'How much cash is in your vault?' Mr Rilcy asked the NBC News interviewer.

'I'm not in a position to answer that question, and I don't have permission from head office to answer those kinds of questions.'

'Would it be right to say millions?'

'I will answer your questions at a later time – no more questions for now. The steel reinforcement is proving very difficult for the drills to go through. They need to be taken out every two minutes and dipped in ice cold water otherwise they will melt.'

Detective Sweeney said to the bank manager, when he came in from the NBC News interview. 'Mr Riley, how much money do we have in that vault?'

'Come into my office, Detective, I don't want anybody to hear us talking.'

Closing the office door Detective Sweeney said, 'Tell me how much money is in the vault.'

'Detective Sweeney, you must not disclose this information as this is a bank secret.'

Mr Riley looked into the eyes of Detective Sweeney with fear. 'Detective, there are millions in that vault.'

'No wonder NBC News was parked across the road on a platform waiting to tell the world what kind the clowns we are. They know something we don't know. They got a tipoff something is wrong with this vault.'

One of the girls knocked at the bank manager's door and entered, 'Sorry, Mr Riley.'

'Yes, girl, come in.'

'Well, they are not working. So now we have another situation,' said Detective Sweeney. 'The electricity doesn't work either. So let's add it up. The vault door should open. The vault is all in darkness, and there are no lights working inside in the vault and that is why it is pitch dark.'

'Yes, Detective Sweeney,' said the bank manager.

Detective Sweeney left the bank with Detective [Rice and] reported back to their boss in the police station. Now [a lot] of people were gathered outside the bank waiting for [news of] the situation. One hour later Detective Rice and S[weeney] returned to the bank with ten detectives.

Detective Sweeney said, 'We are taking over this b[ank as] it is a government national bank.'

'Okay, Detective Sweeney – but don't get in our wa[y as] we have a job to do here as well.'

'Where is that vault technician? Get him for me.' [The] vault technician came over to the Detective. 'I am the lo[cal] Detective Sergeant. What's the story with the vault now?'

'I drilled a hole through the three-foot wall. I put in th[e] lens camera to find absolutely no light in the vault.'

'So you can't see anything?'

'No, just pure black so we have to come up with some other idea.'

'Something is very wrong here in this bank,' said Detective Sweeney to all his men. 'Start asking questions around here discreetly. Especially the vault experts as they might know something. Get an opinion of what could be wrong with that vault door.'

A police van pulled up outside and erected crowd control barriers. They pushed everyone back off the streets to allow the traffic to flow freely. Detective Sweeney and Detective Rice went to the bank manager and said, 'What is your opinion on the vault?' Mr Riley was sweating profusely and under enormous pressure. 'Just tell me what you think.'

'I don't know, Detective. I honestly don't know. But the vault people are saying all the locks are in the open position. There is no reason why that vault door will not open. That is all I can tell you, Detective Sweeney.

'Mr Riley – the vault technician said he inserted the camera lens through the hole in the wall, and all they can see is black, nothing else. So there must be no lights in the vault?'

'Yes, there are lights in the vault, Detective Sweeney,' said to bank manager.

Chapter 22

Twenty-four more hours passed, and the technician had another hole drilled in the vault wall, one he inserted a rod in one hole, the other one he inserted a night vision infrared camera. He set up a twenty-inch flat screen TV connected to the night vision camera. He inserted the rod to push away the black curtain that was hanging around the perimeter of the vault. He said to the assistant vault technician, 'Go get the manager and Detective Sweeney to have a look at this.'

The manager, Detective Sweeney and Rice hurried out of the office and said, 'Show us what you have.'

'Look at the screen when I push away the black curtain.'

The manager and Detective Sweeney were speechless. The fish lens scanned around the whole vault with the manager looking at the TV in shock. They could see the fifty-tonne chain pulling the door closed. They also could see a square hole in the floor and the chain going down into the hole. They could see that the vault was in disarray. Detective Sweeney turned to the bank manager and said, 'How much is gone?'

From looking at that footage, the bank manager turned to Detective Sweeney and Rice and said, 'My God – three quarters of the contents of the vault is gone.'

'How much, Mr Riley?'

'Well, my guess between two and three hundred million.'

'You're fucking shitting me. Three hundred fucking million. You're fucking joking me.'

'I wish I was, Detective Sweeney. I wish I was.'

'You better get out on the street and tell that news crews something.'

'Detective Sweeney, I'm not able, will you please do it for me? I would be grateful.'

'Okay, Mr Riley.'

Detective Sweeney turned around to the other cops that had been accompanying him and said, 'Listen up.' His men quickly gathered around him. 'Right – this is a Tunnel job. There is a Tunnel under the vault. If we can locate it, we can get into the vault and open the door from the inside. So we must find where this Tunnel is coming from. So get out there and search from every direction. Go to every building and check till you find the way out of that Tunnel.'

Detectives ran in all directions with the media asking them what was new with the bank vault but nobody would answer them. Detective Sweeney turned to Mr Riley and said, 'You are famous from this minute. You will go down in history as the biggest bank robbery ever committed is in your bank.'

Detective Sweeney went outside to talk to the media. 'The bank manager asked me to speak to you, so listen up. It looks like we have a Tunnel underneath the bank and underneath the vault. We have viewed the inside of the vault with a night vision fish lensed camera. This was inserted through the walls to see what's going on inside the vault and it looks like this is a huge bank robbery.'

One of the reporters said, 'Could you tell us how much is gone?'

'No, I can't, but take it from me that it's huge. In the history of robberies this one will top them all. I will brief you later as we must find this Tunnel.'

The media turned into a frenzy and flashes the news live around the world.

*

Detective Rice said to Sergeant Sweeney, 'The obvious place to start searching first is the derelict house across the road.'

'You know what, Detective Rice, that is the most intelligent thing I have heard from you since yesterday. Let's get on it.'

Detective Sweeney was so proud that he was the one on TV breaking the news of the biggest bank robbery in history. Now, all he had to do was solve it and he would be the hero of the day. Then he will go down in history as a brilliant cop. On the way across the road the television cameras and reporters stormed around Detective Rice and Sweeney. 'Detectives, give us more information on the bank robbery. Will you please give us some idea of how much money is gone?'

*

Detective Sweeney said in his best TV accent, 'Well, now I hope that he is wrong. Well, blame the bank manager if he is wrong. I asked him to look around the vault shown on the TV with the night vision lens camera and estimate how much money is gone from that vault. And he said there could be up to two hundred million or more missing from the shelving of that vault. Now that is what he said.'

The media went wild shouting into the cameras to be the first to break the news live on TV. You could hear them saying. *This is the biggest robbery in history, this is NBC News,...Sky News...BBC News.* By the end of the day it was on every news station. *A huge bank robbery in Charlestown.*

*

Celine picked up the phone and rang Charlie and said, 'Did you see the news yet?'

'No,' said Charlie.

'On the television, it's all over it.'

'What is it all over it, darling?'

'The National Bank in Charlestown has been robbed of two hundred million.'

'What?'

'That can be true?'
'Where would they get 200 million?'
'It is true.'
'Turn on the TV.'

*

Detective Sweeney and Rice used a shovel to force open the front door of the derelict house and cautiously walked in. They looked in to the front room which had no floor and down into the basement and they could see this was the place.

'There is your Tunnel,' said Detective Rice. 'Look at it over there at the other end of that basement room.'

'Yes, this is it, Detective Rice, this is it. Clear this area. Get it taped off. Get men all over here. We must change into forensic suits before we go down there.'

'I will go get them, Detective.'

*

Charlie hung up the phone to Celine and immediately called Billy.

Billy asked, 'Did you see the news? My town is crawling with TV camera crews. What is going on down there, Charlie?'

'Turn on the news. The National Bank was robbed out of a few million. Wouldn't mind having a share of that, Charlie.'

'Me too, Billy.'

'I will see you for a few drinks when you come down. Okay, over and out for now.' *Well, the story is out now* Charlie thought. *Soon we will know how much money we have when they work out how to get into the bank vault. It shouldn't take them too long to count what's left behind. It's all the small notes. And I also bet a few cops will have plenty drink money if they are doing the counting. Well, anyway it won't make much of a difference for them to have a few free drinks at the cost of the bank.*

Driving around the town centre avoiding the bank area because of the crowds and TV crews having the roads jammed up, Charlie noticed a few of the down and outs had new clothes. And drinking bags of cans down, the back streets on the benches. Some of the wino's faces looked really guilty as if they had all the money from the bank. Charlie looked in the rear-view mirror after passing some of them that had suspicion written all over their faces.

One thing you can count is this: they won't talk and risk losing their Christmas presents. You can be sure each one of them will have their money well hidden somewhere. They will only take out the money they spend for that day in fear of losing it.

NBC News and Sky News had gone insane. They were up in helicopters as well as all over the streets looking for information on the bank robbery.

Detective Sweeney and Detective Rice were climbing down the ladder into the basement of the derelict house. They had on the forensic suits and gloves.

'This is unbelievable,' said Detective Sweeney.

'It's hard to imagine,' said Rice.

They walked up the Tunnel slowly, shining the torches on the structures of the Tunnel. Detective Rice kept repeating himself, 'Unbelievable,' every step he took. 'Unbelievable.'

'Hold the ladder there,' Detective Rice. Detective Sweeney climbed up into the vault and gave a hand to get up Detective Rice. They shone torches around the vault to try and take in the enormity of the situation. They quickly saw the fifty-tonne chain secured to the bars of the door mechanism.

'This is why it won't open. We must get this chain off, Detective Rice.'

'You must go back down the ladder and follow the chain and the steel rope that's going along the Tunnel and open it off whatever it is tied to.'

Detective Rice went back down the ladder and out of the Tunnel to find the attachment to the steel rope and whatever was holding it so tight. 'And Detective – when you get out of the Tunnel ring the bank manager and tell him we are in the vault so try opening the door now when we release it.'

'Okay, Sergeant.' Detective Sweeney was inspecting the handiwork of the Tunnelling gang and was so impressed with the way and the expertise used to gain access to this vault. He was speaking to himself, 'My God what have we here. They pulled up a black curtain all around the vault to slow us down in discovering what was actually wrong. This is the work of professionals.'

Detective Rice found the pulley blocks and managed to release the pressure of the steel rope that had five tonnes pressure on the fifty-tonne chain keeping the vault door closed.

Detective Rice returned to the Tunnel and tracked down the joining of the chain to the steel rope. He unhooked the chain and went back up the ladder into the vault and said, 'Sergeant, the chain is off, pull it up.' Detective Sweeney quickly pulled up the chain and unhooked it from the door bar mechanism. As soon as he did that the door opened and the manager and the vault technicians were waiting to come in. 'Mr Riley, it's all yours now to tell us what's missing,' said Detective Sweeney.

Mr Riley was in total shock. 'My God, look at what they have done.'

'Don't worry what they have done, Mr Riley, worry about what they have taken,' said Detective Sweeney.

'Mr Riley, before you can go back into the vault, I must send in my forensic team, but judging by the smell of bleach that seems to be a waste of time – these people were professionals. They knew exactly what they were doing and they knew exactly how to do it. Looking at the work they carried out, these guys have knowledge of digging Tunnels and the building trade. Mr Riley thinks you better come with me out the front and tell the media what is going on.'

'Okay, Detective – you lead the way.' Detective Sweeney and Mr Riley opened the front door to meet the frenzy of reporters all asking different questions.

Detective Sweeney says, 'Listen up. This is your brief. The bank manager would like to say a few words about this robbery.'

'Hello, ladies and gentlemen – my name is Mr Riley, and I am the bank manager. I wish to inform you that an expert Tunnelling crew dug a Tunnel under the bank from that derelict building across the road to the vault the entered it and removed a couple hundred sacks of money – that is plastic sacks with blocks of cash inside. Some of the cash is used notes and going back into circulation. Also a lot of different foreign currencies, too. I can't put a figure on the total amount stolen but I tell you it's over two hundred million or more. It appears that this job has been carried out by experts. I would like to hand you over to Detective Sergeant Sweeney to tell you a little more about the robbery.'

'First of all, I'd like to say nobody is to enter that derelict property across the road or attempt to enter it. That is a crime scene as from now. I am placing a ring of steel around this town in a thirty-mile radius. No van, car or truck will enter or leave Charlestown or the surrounding area within my cordon without being searched. So expect delays if you intend to travel in or out of Charlestown for the next four weeks.

'The Tunnel was dug from that derelict house right under the road where you're standing. It is right under your feet to the vault and up into the vault. I can't tell you any more technical details for operational reasons because we have just after finding it, but from looking at it, it is the most sophisticated robbery I have ever read about or known of or seen in the movies. We have a lot of work to do. We have a lot of forensics to gather. So if you are patient with us we will brief you as we go down the road with the investigation. At this present moment we don't have any suspects for this robbery. If anybody out there has the slightest bit of information that would help us, please call us on the free phone number we are handing out. I cannot answer any more questions until the investigation progresses – that's all for now.'

Three helicopters flying overhead, one was the police and other two were news helicopters. It was now coming out live on all TV channels that this robbery was the biggest bank robbery in history.

Detective Rice was down in the Tunnel with the forensic team when one of them said, 'Detective Rice, what is this note on the derelict house wall?'

'What does it say?'

'Come see for yourself.'

Detective Rice shone his torch on the wall and could see the message left by the robbers. *"Violence is the whore of the powerless. I came. I took. And I will share. But when I go you will never find me."*

Detective Rice took out his camera and photographed the wall three times. He turned to the forensic team and said, 'These guys are taking the piss. They have robbed all that money and now they are rubbing our fucking noses in it.'

Detective Rice walked down the Tunnel and climbed up the ladder back into the vault where they had removed the black curtain and the lights were now on. He now saw another verse written on the wall of the vault and it said:

"For if you forgive men their trespasses, your heavenly Father will also forgive you, whereas if you do not forgive men their trespasses, neither will your Father forgive your trespasses." Matthew 6:1 14.15.

Detective Rice turned to Detective Sweeney and said, 'Some religious nutcases have robbed this bank.'

'Don't let that fool you, Detective Rice,' replied Sweeney. 'We will find the ones that robbed this bank and then we will see them pray for mercy.'

Charlie, Billy and Mick met in McCarthy's pub just like they met every weekend. The three acted the way they always acted – nothing out of character, giving away no clues. Everyone was looking for clues to who could have possibly committed this huge robbery.

Charlie discreetly said to Billy and Mick, 'The cops are everywhere, lads. Play it cool, only travel on the busses from now on. They have a ring of steel around Charlestown. We know we were searched coming into town, but going out is worse. So park up and use public transport from today on. I don't want ye coming in contact with them cops for any reason.'

'Okay,' said Billy and Mick.

'Now in the pub only talk about the bank if someone else brings it up. Don't get drunk. I will give you some money from the ATM machine across the road when the media circus has gone away for the evening. We will have to wait for at least a week before we can attempt to go near our hiding place. There will be a big reward put in place for information on the robbery in the next couple of days. So it will be more than cops that we have to avoid.'

*

'Gather around,' said Detective Sweeney to all his men in the police station. 'From our initial findings it has become apparent to me that this Tunnel was dug at the same time the bank was built. The concrete floor shows obvious signs that the square that comes up from the Tunnel was constructed at the same time as building the vault floor. So whoever built the new bank vault floor put the cube mould in the floor before the concrete was poured. The robbers only had a few inches to break through instead of three feet.'

'It was O'Brien the builders that had the contract for the whole build,' said Detective Rice. 'And all the Tunnel equipment that was used to support that Tunnel is equipment with O'Brien the builders name on it. Some people might say no foolish man would use his own building equipment to rob a bank.'

'Well, stranger things have happened,' said Detective Sergeant Sweeney.

'Now that just might be the case. Find every person that worked for O'Brien the builders company for the last year.

Trace every piece of equipment to see where it leads back to. Because the equipment used to create that Tunnel and that vault was O'Brien's and that Tunnel was prepared at the time of building the bank. We have enough grounds to go to judge for a research warrant for O'Brien the builders offices and yard. And also for O'Brien's house. We need to find every person that has access to the planning maps of that vault. How could it be possible that someone else made that Tunnel and that vault floor access? It's obvious this is an inside job by the builders. If this trail goes cold, we may not get a second chance to apprehend the Tunnelling gang that committed this huge robbery. We have now got fifty men on this case. So fan out through the town and see can you get any whispers. Somebody must have seen or heard something.'

Detective Sergeant Sweeney was now a household name in Charlestown. But soon his impatience with his own men would hinder his judgement. 'One thing I have to tell you is this. We don't know what day the bank was robbed. It is now a week since the bank closed on Christmas Eve. So they had a week ahead of us. So get the posse and make some progress to try catching up with these cowboys.'

*

It was New Year's Eve and McCarthy's pub was starting to fill up. Charlie, Billy and Mick were there with Celine and her family and two friends. Everybody was enjoying themselves. Nobody in the company was talking about the bank. The news of the robbery has gone cold. Nobody cared for it now. Celine was holding on to Charlie in her romantic way. Billy and Mick were obviously in love with Celine's two friends. Joseph was paying for all the drink because he was looking forward to his daughter getting married early in the New Year.

Celine turned to Charlie and said, 'How do we get married? I'm Jewish and you're Catholic. What do we do?'

'Simple,' Charlie said. 'I will become Jewish or you become Catholic. Or do the church nowadays allow mixed religions to marry without objections?'

'We both believe in the same God,' said Celine.

'Yes,' said Charlie, 'but you don't believe in the son of God, Jesus.'

'Okay.'

Charlie turned and kissed Celine on the forehead and said, 'Darling, it is New Year's Eve, let's not talk about religion in the pub, and we'll sort this out in the week. I will get all the answers for you from Father Condon – he taught me in school. Let's have a happy New Year, darling.'

'Okay, my darling. I will leave it to you. Come back and tell me how we go about getting married.'

'I will, my darling. But one thing – you do the rest, because I can't plan anything. I am useless at that.'

'Okay, my man, I understand.'

Charlie turned to Billy and Mick and said quietly, 'Remind me to go and see Fred the head in the next week.'

'Okay, I will,' said Billy.

*

Back at the police station, they had a meeting and briefed each other every two hours. 'Gather around and listen up,' said Detective Sweeney. 'Right, what have we?'

First one from the team investigating the Tunnel said, 'This is what's happening. We have all the Tunnel equipment Acro props which were used with the scaffolding planks to prop up the Tunnel. We have the miniature rail carriage bins that were used to transport the dirt from the Tunnel. We also have various tools. We have a hydraulic hundred tonne jack which was modified with an extension which we believe they jacked up the floor with. It's obvious that the void in the floor was created by the builders at the time they built that vault. It could not have been done any other way as the concrete was poured onto a cube-type structure that was in the floor before the concrete truck arrived. Now the only ones that could have done that are the builders. It was the same as if they put the mould into the concrete and left a few inches at the top that they concreted over.'

'So what you're saying is that the people that put in the vault floor put in the mould prior to the concrete?'

'Yes, Sergeant Sweeney. It couldn't be done any other way because you can see where the concrete was poured at the same time on top of the cube.'

'Right, next.'

'O'Brien's yard. Nothing yet. We are still searching it, but all the tools and equipment used on the Tunnel belong to O'Brien the builders.'

'Right then – everybody back to work. If you look for me and Detective Rice, we will be in O'Brien's yard and office.' All the detectives went different directions back to go through the evidence. Detective Rice drove an unmarked squad car to O'Brien's the builder's yard and offices trying to avoid the press.

Detective Sweeney said, 'Let's hit the office first.' In the office the two of them were searching through dozens of files building plans and invoices. 'This fucker is not short of money,' said Detective Sweeney.

'Greed is a terrible sin.'

'What is O'Brien saying about searching his house and office?'

'He's pretending to be shocked,' said Detective Rice.

'Well, he's not under arrest yet.'

'We must find something to tie him directly to the robbery. Otherwise he could just say *my staff must've done it*.'

'Sergeant Sweeney – the map of the bank where it is situated is pinned to the wall. It's the area map that goes with every planning permission.'

'Take it down and have a look at it.'

'Yeah, I have, it looks okay. There's just one thing odd about it. When I hold it up to the light.'

'What's that, Detective Rice?'

'There's a little mark on it which is not far from the centre of the map. I never seen anybody mark a map for no reason.'

'Detective Rice – will you look for evidence and not be stupid all the fucking time?'

'Okay, Sergeant – I will go to the town hall and get a copy of the planning permission.'

'Detective Rice, I keep telling to look for evidence.'

'Okay, Sergeant.'

*

Detective Rice put the map with the mark on it in an evidence bag and put it in his pocket. After searching O'Brien's office and yard for an hour Detective Rice and Sweeney headed back to the police station. 'I will be back in ten minutes, Sergeant. Just going down to the shop.'

Detective Rice drove to the town hall and went to the planning office and asked the clerk, 'Can we have the planning application for the bank? I am Detective Rice.'

The clerk said, 'Are you talking about O'Brien's application to build the new bank?'

'That's correct.'

'One moment.' The clerk went to the planning draw and pulled out a brown envelope and handed it to Detective Rice. 'Could you please return that when you're finished, Detective.'

'I certainly will.'

Detective Rice opened the planning application in the hallway of the town hall and pulled out the same area map. He held it up to the light and was gobsmacked. He could see a pinhole in the exact same spot as the mark on the other map. He quickly went to his car and returned to the police station. Detective Rice returned just in time for the next police briefing and update on the robbery.

'Listen up, everybody,' said Detective Sergeant Sweeney. 'I will just give you a brief on what we have. We have a Tunnel dug from the derelict house across the road that's over a hundred and fifty feet long. We have a hole in the vault floor that was cast at the same time as the concrete was laid for that floor. All day equipment was used to create the Tunnel and supported it.'

'Is it equipment belonging to O'Brien the builders?'

'We have a business card of O'Brien's found in the Tunnel. It's obvious where we must start. If it has feathers and it quacks it is a fucking duck. Well, O'Brien the builders is our fucking duck. And the fucking bastard is quacking at us, so fucking pluck the bastard and get answers. We have to start asking questions and making arrests. The first place we start is O'Brien and his builders. This Tunnel was built at the same time as they built the bank. This bank robbery would have been very difficult to carry out if the Tunnel was created after the bank was finished. I want the list of names of everybody that works for O'Brien.'

Detective Rice and Sweeney headed back out to speak to O'Brien the builder's secretary. She said when questioned by Detective Rice, 'Mr O'Brien did say he might fuck off in the New Year, it's just a remark passed, whether it means anything I don't know.'

'Miss, could you look at this map and tell me did you put that mark on that map that was hanging on your wall board.'

'No, I did not. Mr O'Brien hangs up the maps himself.'

'Okay – let me show you another map, it's a copy of the same map which I got from the planning office in the town hall.'

'Yes, Detective.'

'It is the same map. Will you look at this map when I hold up to the light?'

'Okay, Detective.'

'Look at the little pinhole in the middle of the map and just to the left side.'

'Yes, Detective, I see it.'

'Did you put that pinhole in that map?'

'No, Detective, I did not.'

'Okay – have you got the list of names and addresses of all the workers that worked on the bank for the last nine months?'

'Yes, I do have names and phone numbers. But I have no addresses because they are migrant workers from Eastern Europe. And another thing, they're all gone home for Christmas.'

Detective Sweeney intervened and said, 'Miss – you mean to tell me that you have no addresses of these migrant workers and where they might be now?'

'No, Detective, I don't.'

'Is it not your job for tax reasons to have addresses for all your workers?'

'Most of these migrants don't pay tax.'

'Everyone must pay tax, darling,' said Sergeant Sweeney.

'Don't "darling me" Detective, I don't like it. All those workers are subcontractors from other countries that come in and do the work with teams of men, charge a certain price, and then they leave. The use cell phones, and you may not hear from them again. It's a free world and it's not my job to chase people to pay their taxes. I pay my own tax, Detective, and that's all I have to worry about.'

'Thank you for the lesson, miss, you been very helpful. So the only person we can talk to is Mr Noel O'Brien himself.'

'That could be right, Detective.'

Detective Rice cut in, 'Miss, I have to ask you these questions. Do you know anything about the Tunnel in the bank?'

'No, Detective, I don't.'

'Did you hear anything about the robbery of the bank?'

'No, Detective. I didn't hear anything.'

'Did you see anything suspicious going on in the yard or office?'

'No, Detective, I did not.'

'Have you any idea of who could have done this?'

'Detective, I have no idea whatsoever, but I think it's the most exciting thing that has happened in this Charlestown in the last hundred years,' and she laughed out loud.

'Miss, could you look at this business card? Is it one of O'Brien the builder's business cards in this evidence bag?'

'Yes, it is, Detective Rice.'

'Okay, miss, thank you for coming into the O'Brien's office today to help us. If we have any more questions for you, which we don't expect to, we will phone you.'

'Okay, Detective.' As the office girl walked out the front door of O'Brien the builder's office, she turned around and said, 'Detective, Sweeney. If the bank robbers were O'Brien's builders, they kept that secret from me for the last nine months. So I don't expect them to call around and give me a few grand to keep my mouth shut, do you? And another thing, Detective, Mr O'Brien is only a fat slob and smells of body odour.'

'Well, the fat slob that smells of body odour could have robbed the bank,' said Sergeant Sweeney. 'That's all, miss, good afternoon for now.'

When the office girl was gone Detective Sweeney stopped rummaging through all the papers and said to Detective Rice, 'What was all that crock of shit about the fucking hole in the map? And you also went to the town hall to get the planning application from the planning office. Detective Rice, what the fuck are you doing?'

'I just have some kind of the gut feeling that the map is holding a clue.'

'Look, we will get back to it. They don't seem to have any choice, Detective Rice, we will have to arrest O'Brien.'

'Okay, Detective, but let's hold off for another day or two. In a day or two he may not be found. Remember the men are keeping an eye on him.'

'Okay, Detective Rice, we will hold off on arresting O'Brien.'

'Did you notice Detective Sweeney – the secretary doesn't like O'Brien.'

Sergeant Sweeney laughed and said, 'Well, isn't that fucking marvellous, what fucking secretary likes the fucking boss, you dunderhead Rice.'

'Read between the lines, Sergeant Sweeney. She said he's a smelly fatso. And a fat slob. So he must be drooling all over her when she's working in the office. The poor girl.'

'I wouldn't worry about her, Detective Rice. She is well able to talk for herself.'

Chapter 23

'Boys,' said Charlie. 'I am going to pay a visit to the stash just to see that everything is okay. I will do it on my own late tonight.' At the back of Charlie's house there was a river and that river went downstream to the wilderness area where the stash was. Charlie had a canoe with a miniature outboard motor that is run on a car battery. Charlie put the canoe and car battery with the little boat up the back of his shed near the riverbank. At 4 am, Charlie got into the canoe and wired up his silent outboard motor. He saved the battery for going upstream. He put on his night vision helmet. He paddled downstream over two miles and tied up his boat. He creeped to the stash with his night vision helmet on, the type they use in the helicopters. He could see everything around him as clear as day.

It was pitch dark. He quickly made his way to the stash and opened it to find the money right at the top. He took out a few notes to have the look at them. There were fine, they are dry. He took off his little rucksack and stuffed it with cash. It was all fifties and hundreds in used notes. This bit of money was for Mick and Billy to keep them going until the heat died off. He travelled back to his boat at the river bank. He turned on the battery powered outboard motor. The car battery was down at his feet with a permanent wire travelling up and out to the motor. It was connected up to the motor, and he switched it on. He turned the throttle very silently and the boat moved upstream; he locked on the motor throttle with an elastic band, and the rudder was locked straight as well. He helped the boat to gain more speed with his paddle. Now he was travelling upstream faster than he came down. He could see all around him as clear as day.

*

Early the next morning in the police station Detective Rice and Detective Sweeney were going over the evidence of the robbery. Detective Sweeney said to Rice, 'Everything to do with this robbery leads back to O'Brien and his builders. All the equipment is O'Brien's. The builders that built the floor of that bank vault were O'Brien's. Yet we have nothing that we can use to go and arrest O'Brien, because we've no direct evidence to connect him and his office to the robbery.'

Detective Rice was thinking, *My boss is getting very impatient with this investigation. He really wants the glory of solving this massive robbery.*

'Keep O'Brien under 24-hour surveillance and make sure he sees us looking at him. We need to make him sweat.'

'Okay, sir.'

'We just need something to tie him to this robbery.'

'What will we do, Detective Rice?'

'Give me your opinion.'

'Well, if you just give me a couple of hours on the maps and it might bring something in.'

'What are you trying to say, Detective Rice?'

'You keep telling me not to bother with the maps.'

'Okay, Detective Rice.'

'I'll tell you what I'm going to do for you. You're going to be me for the next two hours and I'm going to be you for the next two hours.'

'So, Sergeant Rice – what do you want me to do?'

'Right, Detective Sweeney – call Brian the engineer, and tell him to meet us at Redbridge in twenty minutes. And bring all his surveying equipment with him, as he might need some of it.'

'Okay, Sergeant Rice. I will do what you want.'

Detective Sweeney reluctantly became Detective Rice's go for over the next two hours. Detective Sweeney phoned Brian the engineer and asked him to meet at Redbridge in twenty minutes.

'Right, Sergeant.'

'Rice – let me drive you to Redbridge to meet Brian the engineer.'

'That's fine, Detective. Let's go.'

'Just one minute until I get the maps.'

'Them fucking maps again,' Sweeney said muttering to himself.

Sergeant Rice was driven by Detective Sweeney to Redbridge and waited for Brian the engineer to arrive. Detective Sweeney was very impatient waiting in the car. He felt that this was a complete waste of time.

Along came Brian the engineer, 'Morning Detectives, what can I do for you?'

Detective Rice pulled out a map and laid it out on the roof of his car and said to Brian, 'Look at that pinhole there.'

'Yes,' said Brian.

'Where is that exact spot?' Brian the engineer got out his rule and measured and marked with a pencil and measured again. He said, 'I will show you then. He open the boot of his car and got out what looked like a small bicycle wheel. Okay, detectives. Follow me.'

They walked down the road and got over a gate into a farmer's field. Brian kept walking and looking at his wheel which was clocking up the distances. Detective Rice was right on his heels but Detective Sweeney was sauntering along behind him. When they got to the pinewood grove part of the countryside, Brian give one end of a measuring tape to Detective Rice to stand and hold. While he went off in a direction with his compass, he was talking to himself. 'Right, Detective Rice, over here I have the spot for you.' Detective Sweeney and Detective Rice went over to Brian. Brian pointed at shrubs and said, 'The exact spot on that map is right in the middle of those shrubs.'

So Detective Rice went to the shrubs got down on his knees and crawled in. He noticed a disturbance in the ground underneath his chest. He pulled the shrubs and the sods came away. With that he found the entrance to a hiding place. He was shocked with excitement when he opened the hatch on the tank and could barely speak. 'I have a hideout.'

Detective Sweeney crawled under the bush and looked into the tank and said, 'We have it. We have it, Detective Rice. It's only one hour gone, Detective Sweeney. Am I still Sergeant for another hour.'

'No,' said Detective Sweeney, 'you've done enough.'

'Okay, Sergeant, let's get on to control and get this place sealed off. You stay here Detective Rice and I will go back and get the posse.'

Detective Sweeney turned to Brian the engineer and said, 'I must ask you not to reveal this location to anybody until we get this place sealed off.'

'Okay, Detective, can I go now?'

'Yes, Brian you can go, thank you very much.'

'Thank you very much, Brian,' said Detective Rice from under the bush. 'I don't know what's down in the bunker but something is.'

'Can you get down, Detective Rice, before I go get the team?'

'Yes, there is a ladder inside.'

Chapter 24

Detective Sweeney finally got reception on his cell phone and dialled the police station. When the desk sergeant answered, he said, 'We found the stash, get the men out to Redbridge, you will see our car parked. We are in the field ahead of the car.'

Detective Rice said when he climbed back up the ladder, 'There is no money in the stash. From my cell phone light I could only see empty sacks, plastic sacks and stickers belong to the money.'

Detective Sweeney said, 'O'Brien has moved the money. We now have enough evidence to arrest O'Brien for this robbery. Because that map is from his office and the map from the planning permission has evidence on it that directly links O'Brien to this robbery. I am going to go to the chief to get permission to bring in O'Brien. You stay here, Detective Rice, and take charge of the scene.'

'Okay, Sergeant Detective Rice,' said, but in his mind, he thought, *There goes Detective Sweeney to get the glory from my detective work.*

Detective Sweeney briefed the media outside the police station. 'Listen up you. We have a breakthrough. We found where the money was hidden for a while and then moved on. We have the entire bank's labels and bank sacks that the money was in. I'm sure we will find a lot of forensic evidence in the stash that we have found. I must say this as well. We are now following a definite line of enquiry. Arrests are imminent in this investigation. I expect that this case is about to be solved.'

O'Brien the builder was at home looking at Detective Sweeney make that statement on the news live. He called to the wife. 'Caroline it's on the TV, they have the robbers that robbed the bank.'

'That's good, darling,' she replied. 'So it wasn't you after all.'

'No, darling, it wasn't me.'

'Well, the whole town is whispering that it was you, and your builders.'

'Don't worry, darling, the town gossipers will now have to talk about the real robbers. Detective Sweeney said he is following a definite line of enquiry. So they have the robbers.'

'Okay, my husband, so we are not multimillionaires.'

'I'm afraid not, darling, I'm afraid not.'

Charlie was driving the car when he heard the newsflash coming over the radio that they found the stash and were following a definite line of enquiry. And the robbers will be arrested shortly.

Detective Sweeney was elated with the find of the hiding place in the field. It did not seem to bother him that there was no money in the hiding place.

*

When Detective Rice returned to the station, Detective Sweeney was waiting for him, and ushered him into a room and said, 'We found it together, Detective Rice, didn't we?'

'That's right, Detective Sweeney, we found it together.'

'It was our shared detective work that located that stash.'

'But there's not one banknote in the stash.'

'That doesn't matter, Detective Rice. O'Brien will tell us where it is.'

'Have you arrested him yet?'

'No, we haven't.'

'We will let him think we suspect somebody else until you are ready.'

'You work closely with me, Detective Rice, and we will both come out on top. From now on I will cover your back at all times and you will cover mine.'

'Okay, Sergeant Sweeney.'

'What if O'Brien doesn't talk, Detective Sergeant?'

'He will talk. The evidence is doing the talking for the moment is it not?'

'That's true.'

'They're bringing in O'Brien now,' said Detective Sweeney. The radio had the news live that a man was being arrested for the biggest bank robbery in history. The crowd was outside the police station, and Detective Sweeney was feeding them the information they required. 'Myself and my colleague Detective Rice went searching out the country and found a hiding place by our own detective work. I feel this case is about to break open in the next couple of hours, and we should be able to locate the money. This was a highly technical robbery carried out by expert builders. But no matter how good you are if we find a crack, we will prise it open. And that's what we are just about to do. But that's it for now, have to go and see what the prisoner has to say.'

'Where is the money, Detective Sweeney?' asked a reporter.

'Be patient, we will let you know when we have it.'

Detective Sweeney asked the questioning detectives what O'Brien was saying. 'All he's saying is he knows nothing about the robbery. He is laughing at the fact that he is arrested for it. But I think that O'Brien is very nervous that's why he's laughing, Detective Sweeney.'

'That's another thing, Detective Rice, the bank manager called and said two hundred million is gone and small change.'

'This is getting better,' said Detective Sweeney.

Detective Rice said, 'Did you ask the bank manager how much he put away for next summer's holidays out of the vault with a laugh?'

'I'm only joking, Detective,' said Rice walking into the interview room with Detective Sweeney, where O'Brien was being questioned. Detective Sweeney said to the interviewing detective without even looking at O'Brien, 'Did you tell him he's looking at twenty-five years and he will not survive.'

'I think he knows that, Detective Sweeney.'

'That is big time. I see the smile is gone off your face, Mr O'Brien. I'm Detective Sweeney and this is my investigation. Mr O'Brien I am making you one offer. You make a statement admitting you were the organiser of the robbery. Your builders did it for you. If you give back all the money I will talk nicely to the judge when you go to court. Then you will only get ten years with five suspended. Otherwise, going up the river for 25 years. You will not get a better offer than this.'

'Detective Sweeney, I did not do this robbery. And I played no part in the robbery. I don't know anything about the robbery.'

'Mr O'Brien, we have you caught. So when you are caught, you are caught.'

'No you haven't, Detective.'

'We have enough evidence to tie you to this crime, and we are now going to tell you. We have evidence that all the equipment used in this robbery which would be a truckload of equipment was all from your building yard. Your name is on every piece of equipment used in the robbery. Over 200 Acro props. Over two hundred planks that were holding up the Tunnel with your name is stamped all over them. And in your yard are the same Acro props and the same scaffolding planks with your name written in the same way.'

'It might be my equipment, Detective, but I didn't do the robbery.'

'You didn't report a truckload of equipment stolen from your yard – did you forget, Mr O'Brien?'

'Well, it's easy to say someone stole it all out of your yard. But we also found evidence in your office which ties you directly to this robbery. But that we won't tell you for now. And in the Tunnel was one of your business cards. You're not saying much now, O'Brien, you're keeping your cards close to your chest, aren't you?'

Celine phoned Charlie and told him that they arrested O'Brien the builder for the bank robbery.

'I know, darling, I was listening to it on the news. Darling, I was talking to Father Condon in St. Peter and Pauls. He said a Jewish girlfriend can marry in his cathedral church downtown.'

'Oh, my darling, I love you, and can't wait until you are my husband.'

'I love you too. I must go now. I have a bit of work to do.'

Back at the police station the questioning of O'Brien was getting nowhere and Detective Sweeney said to Detective Rice, 'Well, if you robbed two hundred million and took nine months to dig the Tunnel and prepare for it, you'd have to pay off all the workers to do it for you.'

'Would you talk, Detective Rice?'

'I suppose I wouldn't, Sergeant.'

'Well, neither will he. No matter what kind of a fat smelly bastard he is. Did you notice Detective Rice the office girl was right?'

*

The next day, O'Brien the builder was taken to court and remanded in custody. Detective Sweeney gave evidence to the judge and said, 'I have enough evidence to tie Mr Noel O'Brien to this robbery of the National Bank. I believe a reasonable minded jury would convict him unanimously.'

'What about bail, Detective, for Mr O'Brien?'

'Under no circumstances would I agreed to bail in this case, because of the enormous amount of money involved, over two hundred million is missing from that vault and we need to get that back. The only chance we have I believe is to keep Mr O'Brien in custody while we are investigating the whereabouts of the money.'

'Okay, Detective, I've heard enough. From what Detective Sergeant Sweeney has said to me under oath leaves me no choice but to remand Mr Noel O'Brien in custody to be brought before me again in seven days or less. The court rests.'

Outside the courthouse, Detective Sweeney was giving another briefing to the TV crews. He was glorifying himself in the investigation. 'Listen up, everybody. We have charged a local builder, Mr Noel O'Brien, for this robbery, because we have the evidence to charge him. He is still denying it. But the evidence is too strong and will hold up that denial. We expect he will come and put his hands up and give back all the money in a matter of days. I would like to thank all my investigating team for the efforts they put into this investigation. And especially I'd like tank my partner, Detective Rice, for his painstaking work with me in cracking open this case.'

Detective Rice shied away from the crowd without Detective Sweeney noticing he was gone.

*

Charlie phoned the prison to book a visit to see Fred the head in the middle of the week. When Detective Rice was driving through the back streets, he noticed that the winos were still shying away from his car when they saw it coming. He reported this to Detective Sweeney who said, 'Take no notice of those bums. They will tell you lies trying to get the price of the next bottle of wine.'

'But have you not noticed, Detective Sweeney, they are dressed very well since Christmas?'

'Yeah, Detective Rice. The families buy clothes for the down and outs for Christmas because they feel sorry for them.'

*

It's now a couple weeks since the robbery and everything was going to plan the way Charlie thought it out. The search of the tank in the field was completed and removed out of the ground. Not one single banknote was found in the tank. They had nothing yet.

Five days passed with O'Brien in prison. 'It's not looking so good for you,' said his wife on the visit to see him. 'Noel,' she said crying, 'just give back the money and things will be all right. Tell me where the money is, and I will see to it that it is found.'

With tears in his eyes looking at his wife, he said, 'Even you think I stole that money. Well, I did not, and if you don't believe me you get away from me now and get out of here. Get out, get out,' O'Brien kept shouting at his wife.

She stood up starting to walk to the door shouting back, 'You must have some other woman who you're going to run off with to spend the money.'

'Don't come back, you bitch.' O'Brien was restrained by the officers and was screaming at his wife as she left. O'Brien was cracking up. The prison officers dragged him off the visit and put him in the segregation unit. He was now on suicide watch. He was now in the block where only Fred the head lived with his cats. The prison officer said to O'Brien, 'Any more of that kind of incident on a visit and you will not be getting any more visits from anybody.'

Fred the head was called for a visit as the officers put O'Brien in the segregation cell. Fred the head turned to O'Brien and said as they closed the door, 'If you can't do the time, don't commit the crime,' and started laughing, walking to his visit.

Fred was called to go to visiting Box 3. Charlie was standing there waiting for him. Fred leaned over the table and shook Charlie's hand and said, 'How is my old friend?' in his curse Scottish accent.

'I am fine, Jock, how are you?' Charlie said to him loud enough for the officer to hear him.

'I came up to tell you to help an old family friend, Mr Noel O'Brien, who was remanded in custody for the two hundred million bank robbery. Nobody believes he has done it, Jock,' Charlie remembering not to call him Fred because that was his mad nickname. Charlie sat down and Fred pulled his chair closer to Charlie. 'Did you get the money I sent you, Jock?'

'I did, Charlie, thank you very much, it all goes on cat food.'

'I will send you a parcel of socks, shoes and boxers in the week.'

'You're a very kind man, Charlie.'

'Jock, do you want to leave this prison for good and get on with your life on the outside?'

'I'm here thirty years now, and I have no way of living on the outside. All because I have over thirty cats and I'm not leaving them behind. If I go, they will have the cats removed and put to sleep. I could not afford a place that I can bring all my cats to.'

'Jock, look at me,' said Charlie. Jock looked into Charlie's eyes and Charlie could see pure sadness on Jock's face.

Chapter 25

Charlie could see that Fred the head wanted to leave prison but could not because it would break his heart to leave his cats behind. 'Fred, sorry, Jock.'

'You can call me Fred like the rest of them, Charlie.'

'Okay, Jock, I will call you Fred. If you had a country house with a few acres of land and big barns to house your cats in and plenty money to take care of them – would you leave prison then?'

'Charlie, of course I would. I am not institutionalised regardless of what they say about me. The only reason I tell them I could not cope on the outside is because they would put me out and I would lose my cats.'

'Fred, I will give you everything you need to live on the outside with your thirty cats. You will never need to worry about the money to take care of them.'

'Charlie when I met you in the boiler house when you were here for that short time. I knew you were a good man when I saw all my cats jumping up on your lap to be groomed. That was it, Charlie, my cats know good men. I can pick out an evil animal like some of those over on the main wing.'

'The real reason I'm here, Fred, is O'Brien killed my fiancée's pet cat, he threw petrol on it and lit it. The poor animal screamed to death. O'Brien also robbed my father-in-law out of a lot of money. But I forgave him.'

'What, O'Brien killed your fiancée's cat!'

'Yes, he did.'

'O'Brien was just pulled off a visit for screaming at his wife. He was just put in the segregation unit which is my block when I was coming out to your visit.

'I must go, Charlie, O'Brien is on my block with my cats and they might let him out of the cell. I should have noticed my cats were running down the landing when they heard his voice when they were dragging him to the segregation cell.'

'Fred, give me six weeks to organise a place for you to live with your cats for the rest of your life. I will arrange to come up here with an Ivor Williams trailer with thirty cages on it to take your cats and you to your new home. So, Fred, start telling the prison authorities and welfare officers that you're ready to leave prison and bring all your cats with you.'

'I could go today if I wanted to, Charlie. I don't need to give them notice, they would be glad to get rid of me. They only keep me in the boiler house to keep me away from the scumbags on the main wing, because I would not put up with them.'

Fred leaned over the table and whispered in Charlie's ear. 'I really appreciate what you're going to do for me. Now I will see that O'Brien escapes up the fucking chimney like the rest of them did.'

Charlie never answered Fred the head but gave him a look straight in the eye, saying, 'You take care of business.' Fred the head winked and walked away.

Charlie shouted after him, 'That cat's home wants you to work for them.'

Fred smiled and hurried away.

*

Fred was up early the next morning. His cell was never closed. He was a total trustee because they wanted him to go home but he would not.

In came the staff member to look in on O'Brien. 'Good morning, Jock.'

'Good morning to you to, sir.'

The officer was looking in on O'Brien. 'You kept me awake all night coming in and out keeping an eye on him.'

'I know, Jock, can't be helped. Between you and me he is cracking up.'

'So would you, sir, if you had two hundred million and were locked up?'

'I suppose I would, Jock.'

'Leave the door open and I will look after him. I will get him to help me in the boiler house.'

'Okay, Jock, keep an eye on him for me. I don't want him found swinging from a sheet.'

'Don't worry, sir, leave him to me. A hard day's work in the boiler house shovelling turf into the furnace will take all the worries out of his head very fast.'

'Okay, Jock, you look after him.'

Fred went into O'Brien's cell. 'Come on, Mr O'Brien, out of bed man. You are with me now on boiler house duty sonny.'

So Fred spent a day in the boiler house with O'Brien keeping one eye on him and the other on his cats. 'You can call me Fred like the rest of them.' Fred was getting to know O'Brien.

That night it was only Fred and O'Brien on the old block and O'Brien's door was left open. Jock went to the door and said good night to O'Brien and pulled out the door and closed it because he couldn't trust him around his cats.

Jock went back to his own cell and took down his big old black coat and put it on and a scarf around his face and pulled down a big woolly hat over his ears. He retrieved his old master key that he had for the last ten years. He headed for the abandoned back gate and slipped in the key in the wicket and slipped out locking it behind him. He hurried down the street with the wind and rain blowing in his face; it was so dark he couldn't see his feet. This was ideal for Fred's visits down to the local pub. He sat in his quite little snug where nobody took any notice of him, but a lot of people in the pub knew who Jock was. To them he was a gentleman. Some of the staff sent up a drink from time to time. Before the evening drew to a close Fred slipped out as quietly as he slipped in. The next day the governor called the meeting and told all the staff, 'We must keep O'Brien away from the prison population, because if any of the prisoners get him to tell them where the money is, after they locate the money O'Brien would be killed to prevent him from telling the police. They will pressurise him to tell where it is. So keep him over in the old segregation block with Jock. Give them whatever they want to keep them happy.'

Only the staff called him Jock, the prisoners all called him Fred the head. Fred the head got O'Brien out of bed early again. He made him eat a big breakfast fry-up he got over from the kitchen. 'Right Mr O'Brien, we have work to do.' They went to the boiler house. 'Yesterday was your introduction day but today is real work. So you watch the way I do this and then you can do it for as long as you want.'

Fred opened the hatch on the boiler with his fork, and said, 'Never put your hands on any part of the boiler, you will stick to it, red hot.' Using the big six-pronged fork, Fred shovelled the turf into the furnace and used a long bar with a square plate to push it in the back. He then closed the door and rounded up another pile of turf. The same thing again: opened the door shovelled in six loads. Pushed it all to the back and close the door. 'It's simple, Mr O'Brien.'

'Okay, Jock.'

'No, you don't call me Jock, you call me Fred like all the other prisoners do. Only staff call me, Jock.'

'You can call me, Noel.'

After two hours O'Brien was physically wrecked from shovelling the turf into the furnace. Fred said in his Scottish accent, 'Okay, laddie, you rest now.' Fred opened his little fridge and took out two ice cold bottles of Guinness. He pulled the corks with his teeth, and handed one to O'Brien. 'Because you work in the furnace you need a lot of iron. The heat and the hard work will drain the energy out of you laddie. So my allowance every day is three bottles of Guinness. But now I will ask for that to be doubled for you.'

O'Brien said to Fred, 'I'm so grateful to you for you looking after me.'

'Don't worry about that, laddie.' At noon, just like always, the staff member arrived at the boiler house with lunch for Fred and his new helper. In a bag he had six bottles of Guinness. Fred turned round to O'Brien and said, 'See I told you – we will be looked after when you work hard with me.'

'I didn't rob the bank, Fred.'

'I don't want ta know about that, Noel, if you robbed the bank or na laddie. When you're here it doesn't matter how much money you have outside. You still have to work as if you had nothing. Money makes very little difference to your life in prison.'

'Have you any advice for me, Fred?'

'All say is this – I see a lot of men coming and going from this place, and the biggest problem they have is this. They can't keep their mouth fucking shut. They trust very easily when they're at their weakest moment. That is when it all tumbles down for them. Guilty or innocent, you keep your mouth shut at all times.'

'I will, Fred. I will keep my mouth shut.'

After a hard day's work in the boiler house, O'Brien was in the shower looking up at the ceiling that hadn't been painted for a hundred years. Everything was rusty. Reality was starting to set in. O'Brien heard the jingling keys of the officer coming along with the clean prison kit that he will receive once a week. The dull grey flaking painted brick work tortured O'Brien's mind thinking he could be in this for ever. When he was washed, he returned to the old dreary grey cell which was so dark he had to turn on the lonely twenty-five-watt bulb in the daytime. Every time he closed the door, he could hear the metal sound that sent a shiver up his spine.

*

Charlie went to a solicitor up the country and asked him to purchase a property he had in mind for Fred the head, 'I want you to buy this property in trust for a man called Fred Moran. I will send you a cheque to cover all costs. I don't want Mr Fred Moran to know who bought the property – that is to be kept secret, so for that reason I will not disclose my name. He's an old member of my family, that's all you need to know.'

'Okay, sir – I will take care of that. What is Mr Moran's address?'

'I don't want you contacting Fred Moran. I will call in to see you in two weeks for the deeds and your cheque will be on the way tomorrow.' The pressure was piling on now that Charlie had to sort out this money, and two hundred million was a lot of sorting.

*

O'Brien was back in court again. Mr Lennon stood up, 'Your Honour. I am representing Mr O'Brien as from today. I am applying for Mr O'Brien to be released on bail pending his trial.'

'Yes, Mr Lennon,' said the judge.

The prosecution said, 'I'd like to call Detective Sweeney to give evidence on behalf of the prosecution.' Detective Sweeney was sworn in.

'I am still objecting to bail for a number of reasons, Your Honour. One is the money has not been located yet. Also we have evidence suggesting Mr O'Brien has split up with his wife and has no fixed abode. In other words, Your Honour, Mr O'Brien has no reason to stay around here anymore.'

Mr Lennon jumped to his feet, 'I must object to Detective Sweeney's evidence, Your Honour. Firstly, my client Mr O'Brien has the presumption of innocence at all times prior to being convicted by a jury of his peers. I would ask Detective Sweeney to keep that in mind prior to a conviction. Also the private life of my client should not be thrown around this court. As this is hearsay, and hearsay in law has no bearing on the court.'

The prosecutor quickly jumped to his feet. 'Your Honour, we have a lot of solid evidence that the equipment used in the Tunnel was all O'Brien's and some paperwork was found in his office that connects directly to where the bank wrappings and sacks were hidden in a secret hide out in the countryside.

For this reason the evidence is not just circumstantial or rumour based on hearsay – this is solid evidence. I ask Your Honour to continue to remand Mr Noel O'Brien in custody for this robbery.'

'Okay, I have heard submissions from both sides. The evidence is damming to say the least. My feeling is this: the evidence the police have is a smoking gun to this robbery and it does connect back to the accused. The presumption of innocence will remain until otherwise changed by the jury of his peers. Two hundred million is a lot of money for our national bank to loose. Now the accused is innocent in law at this time. But just say that there is a chance that O'Brien does have this enormous amount of money. To give him bail and risk losing a chance of getting that money back is a risk I am not willing to take. Now if somehow the police located all this money – that would be a game changer for his bail application that could be lodged in my court at any time. And then I would look more sympathetically at Mr O'Brien's situation. But in the meantime, we have enough evidence to continue remanding him in custody pending his trial. This is my finding. The court rests.'

Chapter 26

Mr Lennon went back to his office after O'Brien was remanded in custody again. His partner, Mr Smith, asked him, 'What have they on our O'Brien that he didn't give him bail today?'

'Well, they have a lot of equipment that was used in the construction of the Tunnel with his name on it, and they also have a map that had a pinhole in it in his office and the same mark was on the map in the town hall planning application. And these were handled only by O'Brien, the prosecution are saying, because there's no other fingerprints on the maps, only O'Brien's. They found a hiding place with all the bank sacks in it and that place was the hole on the map.'

'So what you're telling me is he put a hole in his own map of where he stashed the money.'

'It looks like that's what he did. But the money was moved very quickly. In reality it took a good cop to find that hide by finding the hole on that map.'

'Which cop found it?'

'From the grapevine I hear it was that young Detective Rice that found it, but Sweeney is taking the credit.'

'As they do, Mr Lennon. It's another case of the tail wagging the dog.'

'What is O'Brien saying about this, Mr Lennon?'

'He said he knows nothing about the bank robbery.'

'And you believe him?'

'Well, I have to take what is my client's word.'

'I asked you a question. Do you believe him?'

'To be honest I have my doubts. But I have to defend him in every possible way I can.'

'Well, Mr Lennon, if I stole two hundred million and got away with it, I wouldn't talk either, would you?'

'It's a lot of money. I know that O'Brien was told he is looking at twenty-five years hard time. But that's a lie. He's only looking at ten maximum and if he gave back all the money, he is looking at seven.'

'How do you know, Mr Lennon?'

'He doesn't know all this and he is playing the game.'

'Did he offer you one million here or one million there to get off?'

'No, he didn't, Mr Smith.'

'Well, then he is one clever bastard keeping his cards to his chest. So Mr Lennon, the cops believe that Mr O'Brien got his migrant workers to build the bank and, in the process, the migrant workers built the Tunnel for Mr O'Brien and also robbed the bank for him as well. So where are all the migrant workers?'

'I know, Mr Lennon. They all went home for Christmas and did not return since. I'm sure they saw the robbery investigation on the news. You will never see them again whether they did it or not.'

'So, if you remove the evidence of the map in O'Brien's office the rest against him is circumstantial.'

'That's true, Mr Smith, but that one piece of evidence is the twister in this case. That alone will convict him.'

'I agree, Mr Lennon.'

*

Back in prison the next morning O'Brien was up and out of bed, getting used to prison life and settling in. He knew the drill now of keeping the furnace going in the boiler house. Dinner time came and Fred set up a make shift table and got an old sheet for a table cloth. They had plastic mugs, knives and forks and some toilet paper for napkins. Along came the dinner as usual; Fred put a rag apron.

Fred opened a bottle of Guinness and half filed his plastic mug and turned to O'Brien and said, 'Would you like to taste the wine, sir.'

'I will, waiter, if you don't mind,' said O'Brien. O'Brien sipped the Guinness from the plastic mug and said, 'Yes this is a very good 1961 Beaujolais, thank you waiter.' Fred put O'Brien's lamb chop on the plate and garnished it with peas and carrots. 'Everything to your liking, sir,' said Fred.

'Yes, waiter – the steak is very tender,' said O'Brien eating it from his fork.

'Okay so, may I join you, sir, now that you're on your own?'

'Yes, pull up a chair, waiter, and have a steak on me with some '61 Beaujolais.'

'I will if you don't mind, sir.' When they had finished their chops Fred turned to the dish and scooped out some rice pudding onto the dinner plates as they had no desert bowels. 'Do you like your chocolate fudge desert garnished with ice cream, prunes, dates and chocolate?'

'Yes, waiter. Tell the chef the food is excellent.'

As they drank their Guinness from the plastic mugs, both of them were in stitches laughing. A member of staff was around the corner and could hear the banter going on in the boiler house. He later pulled Jock and said, 'You cheered O'Brien up, Jock.'

'I have done that, sir. I have.'

*

Billy and Mick were in Eastern Europe picking out properties that they could buy for cash with no questions asked. Charlie was with Celine in the wedding dress shop, Celine was buying the dress but he couldn't see it. This is the one thing every man does under protest but don't dare say one word of boredom.

*

It was three weeks now since the robbery and the media had died down but they were still lurking in the shadows waiting for something else to break. They want to know where the money is.

Charlie booked another visit to see Fred the head. The next morning Charlie arrived in prison early for the first visits. Fred came out all full of smiles and happy. 'How are you, Charlie?'

'I'm good, Fred.'

'How are you, Fred? And what's more, how is O'Brien?'

Fred the head leaned across the table and said, 'O'Brien is my best friend. He is working in the boiler house with me. I am looking after him in the derelict segregation wing. Because the Governor is worried that O'Brien could tell inmates where the money is and then he would be killed to silence him. So he is over with me.'

'What is the story with him?'

'I have the entire plan in motion. I will have got rid of him in the next week, so don't be worried, he will be gone.'

'Okay, Fred, the solicitor has the property bought. I'm collecting the deeds next week and going to visit the property and get the place ready for your homecoming. I will have the barn converted for your cats. They won't be long getting used to the place, it's lovely. I have some photographs here to show you.' Charlie handed Fred the photographs which he looked at and admired every one of them.

'I don't know how I'm ever going to pay you back, Charlie.'

'There is no payback. Only the favour to get rid of O'Brien.'

'What is the story anyway? I wish I could do more for you. O'Brien will be gone.'

'O'Brien is a fat slob, you will have your work cut out putting him into the furnace on your own.'

'Leave my job to me, Charlie. He will be taken care of.'

'I'm getting married, Fred, to the girl I told you about. Celine said you're invited to the wedding which will be in a few weeks.'

'I look forward to that, Charlie.'

'The next time I see you, Fred, I will have a jeep with an Ivor Williams trailer and thirty cages strapped down. I have permission to drive in the main gate and over to the boiler house to load up your cats. So make sure all them cats are rounded up that morning.'

'I will, Charlie. I will have them all ready to go to their new home.' Fred shook Charlie's hand and didn't want to let go. 'See you soon, Fred.'

'God be with you, Charlie.'

*

Back at the police station, two chief cops arrived from the city to see Detective Sweeney. They entered the office and said, 'No need for introductions, Detective Sweeney, you know who we are. I will get to the point. You Detective Sweeney are lead investigator in this case. Are you making arrests of the suspects of this robbery?'

'Yes, we have the main suspect in prison on remand as you know.'

'Detective Sweeney – do you think that O'Brien dug the Tunnel all by himself. Did he put in the vault floor mould cube on his own before the cement was poured? Of course you don't.'

'No, I don't, but I'm sure he got his workers to do it for him. I am following this definite line of enquiry. The other suspects are out of reach, gone back to Eastern Europe for Christmas. I don't have the information I need to arrest the other suspects.'

'The truth is you don't know who these men were.'

'I know for sure O'Brien is the ringleader of this robbery.'

'So, what you're saying, Detective Sweeney, is, it looks like O'Brien the builder got his workers to dig the Tunnel at the time they were renovating the bank and he provided all his own equipment to do so.'

'That's correct, Chief – you have it there all in one.'

'Well, I can tell you now, Detective Sweeney, it looks like it. Do not get convictions from a jury. Speculation, that is all you have. Speculation is for Wall Street, Detective Sweeney.'

'With all due respects, Chief, I have cracked this nut, and I will pull it apart, sir.'

Chief Murphy turned to the other chief and said, 'This is Chief McDonough. And he is a witness to what you just said. You crack the nut.'

'Well, Detective Sweeney, I must warn you. Don't let this nut crack your career. Fuck up on this, Detective Sweeney, and you're history. You do know that don't you, Detective Sweeney?'

'Yes, sir. I do know that.'

'Detective Sweeney – make sure you keep your revolver in the draw and a bottle of whiskey close by. You might have to do the honourable thing.'

'I get the message, sir.'

'Right, Detective Sweeney, we are out of here. Best to luck with your investigation.'

'Thank you, sir.'

The two top cops left the building and drove away in a black jeep with blacked out windows. One chief said to the other as they drove away, 'Detective Rice is the only one in that cop shop with brains.'

'I agree, sir,' said the other.

As Sweeney looked out the window at them driving away, he muttered to himself, 'Fucking Gestapo bastards. Who the fuck do they think they are?'

*

Billy and Mick arrived back from their mission in Eastern Europe where they compiled a portfolio of properties. They met in Charlie's house. Sitting at the table having lunch, they passed around some photographs of the properties, apartments, business properties and price lists.

'How did you get on over there?' asked Charlie.

'Well, it's like this,' said Mick. 'The only thing that talks in those countries is cash. They would eat you for cash when you tell them that I have lots of cash to invest in properties.'

'What are the estate agents saying?'

'They were genuflecting to us. They could not do enough for us. They drove us around to see really high-quality apartments and high-quality offices which were a very reasonable price when you compare it to here.'

'Did you go and see solicitors?'

'Yes, we did,' said Billy. 'We sussed out a few English-speaking solicitors and we gently put it to them that we are interested in investing in a lot of money in their country. They were over the moon when they heard us say we want to buy in cash.'

'That's good.'

'Can we trust them?'

'Well, we said to one solicitor, who is an expert in worldwide law on property, and we told him we would pay him to make sure everything was done for us above board. We also told him we would be taking documents out of the country to be verified by a legal team in another country to make sure they were not trying to scam us.'

'That is good,' said Charlie. 'It's time to take out some of the money and bag it up for transport.'

'I told you about the plane I have in the garage down the back of the house.'

'Charlie you did mention the plane and that you had a pilot's licence, that's all you said.'

'Right, I will explain it to you now. I have a small three-seater plane that has been modified so that the wings can be removed. In other words, my plane is a Cri-Cri hybrid fold-up plane and can be carried in horse box without anybody noticing it. It is the smallest plane in the world that a person can get into and fly. Also, my plane has a hybrid engine. That means it runs on batteries as well as petrol. The reason for this is I can take off and land by battery power in silence and turn on the petrol engine when in the sky. Now down the back of my house is the riverbank which you've seen a number of times. Did you notice it has a grassy bank that's five hundred yards long going downstream? The grass is a bit high so I'm going to borrow a big tractor lawnmower and cut the grass all the way down to five hundred yards so that I can take off and land on the riverbank. There are no high trees in the vicinity and no power lines crossing the land. Nobody owns this land so nobody can complain. So we're going to start moving the money from the hideout up the river in a boat, onto the plane and fly out of the area over the ring of steel. So that's the plan. Now we will be moving it in the next few days.'

'What's happening with O'Brien while we were away?'

'O'Brien is remanded in custody because they found the map in his office with the hole in it and the map in the town hall with the same. So that ties them directly to the Tunnel.'

'The maps were the planning permission to renovate the bank. So that's why you put the hole in the map, Charlie?'

'Yes, it was. All in good time, all in good time, remember.'

'Now I get it,' said Billy.

Chapter 27

The following night Billy and Mick returned to Charlie's house. Charlie had spent all day cutting the grass on the riverbank. It was a pitch-dark night and Charlie's house was in a fairly secluded area. The three men went down the field to the shed down the very back of the house. Charlie had the plane out and the wings assembled.

Billy said, 'My God – how are we going to go up in that?'
'You don't have to if you're scared of flying,' said Mick.
'I will go up with Charlie.'
'Help me push the plane and we will go for a test flight in it now.'
'In the dark?' said Billy.
'Yes, why not?' said Charlie.
'Can you fly in the dark?'
'Don't I have a night vision helmet that I can see in the dark with?'
'Okay – will it take the three of us?' asked Mick.
'Just about,' said Charlie. They pushed the plane and lined it up with the river bank, and Charlie said, 'All aboard,' when they were all strapped in.

Charlie put on his night vision helmet and pressed the button for the hybrid engine to use batteries only on take-off. Slowly the plane started to move down the riverbank. Charlie said, 'Everybody hold on, here we go.' Charlie revved the engine to full throttle. The plane raced down the riverbank. Charlie pulled back on the stick and the plane lifted off the grass on battery power with no engine noise and she slowly climbed into the sky.

At about three hundred feet Charlie steered the plane over to the wilderness area and switched over to the petrol engine.

Suddenly, the plane had lots of power. Billy and Mick were stuck to their seats with fear. 'I don't blame you for being scared up here at night time. We will just turn around and take it back down.' Charlie lined up the plane for the landing and turned off the petrol engine to land on batteries. The plane slowly came down silently and landed on the grass, rolled up the riverbank for a very short distance and came to a stop.

Billy and Mick made signs of relief when the plane landed. 'That was awesome,' said Billy.

'It freaked me out,' said Mick, 'and I was the one that volunteered instead of Billy.'

The three men pushed the plane back to Charlie's big shed. Charlie got out some tools and removed the bolts on the wings and the wings folded back. They pushed the plane over to the corner of the shed and put the black polythene over it. 'Tomorrow night, as soon as it gets dark, we are moving the first ten million. I will fly the plane on my own two hundred and fifty miles to a private estate. Because of the weight of the money it cannot carry the money and all of us.'

'Thank fuck for that,' said Billy.

'You can say that again,' said Mick.

'What kind of plane is that?' asked Billy.

'It's a Cri-Cri hybrid plane modified with folding wings and hybrid engine. I must put the batteries on full charge for take-off again tomorrow night.'

*

Early the next morning, a newsflash came on the television. It was NBC News. 'Reports are just coming in that the man charged with the biggest bank robbery in history has vanished from prison. We are coming to you live from outside Edison prison. We are going to speak to the governor now. Governor, could you throw some light on the latest development in your prison?'

'Yes, we can confirm that at 8 am this morning, Mr Noel O'Brien was not in his cell. For his own protection, we kept him over in the segregation unit along with a long-term prisoner.'

'Have you any idea where Mr O'Brien is?'

'I have no idea what so ever. But I can say if you have two hundred million at your disposal you could have a lot of things done. All his belongings that he came to prison with are still in his cell.'

'Was his cell locked last night?'

'Yes it was and checked at midnight and he was there.'

'Is there any way Governor Mr O'Brien could be hiding in the prison grounds?'

'That is not possible, we have searched every inch of Edison prison this morning.'

'Well, that's it from NBC News. It's now confirmed that the man that allegedly robbed two hundred million from the National Bank in Charlestown has vanished. We now go live to Charlestown to speak with Detective Sergeant Sweeney. Hello this is NBC News in Charlestown. We are speaking here to Detective Sergeant Sweeney in charge of the investigation of the two hundred million robbery of the National Bank. Detective Sweeney – what have you to say about Mr O'Brien going missing?'

'Well, it proves one thing which I was always sure and certain of – Mr O'Brien is the one that master minded the robbery of the bank. An innocent man doesn't run. And Mr O'Brien has proved he is guilty beyond all doubt. And I have no doubt that his migrant workers dug the Tunnel on Mr O'Brien's instructions. They returned and freed him from prison. Prisons are built to keep men in, not out. It's obvious people went in over the walls and extracted O'Brien out of Edison prison. We will leave no stone unturned to bring Mr O'Brien and his Tunnel team to justice.'

Back inside the police station, Detective Sweeney saw his fate in front of his eyes. 'If they don't find O'Brien in twenty-four hours my fate is sealed. I'm history.'

Detective Sweeney turned to Detective Rice and said, 'I'm fucked.' Detective Rice looked at Sweeney and put his head down in silence. The chief came in and said to Sergeant Sweeney, 'What have you done now that O'Brien is gone?'

'Absolutely nothing, sir.'

'So you backed all your chips on O'Brien breaking and coughing up the money. You really thought he was going to break and give you the list of the names that dug the Tunnel on his instructions?'

'I did, sir.'

Back at the prison the Governor was talking to Jock. 'I didn't hear a thing from the time I went to sleep last night to the time I heard the news that O'Brien was gone. I went over to the kitchen to get the old milk for my cats. When I came back the officers were searching everywhere for O'Brien. I na oot aboot it. O'Brien going missing. He never telt me oot about his escaping.'

*

The Governor said, 'Jock – Detective Sweeney leading this case is on his way to see you. He should be here in a few minutes to see if you can shine and a light on the bank robbery.'

'Okay, Governor – I will help Detective Sweeney in any way I can.' Ten minutes later Jock was called for a visit from Detective Sweeney. 'Hello, Jock – how are you keeping?'

'I'm fine, Detective – what can I do for you?'

'It's about O'Brien – can you help me in any way about how they got out of prison?'

'Sir, I told the Governor this morning everything I knew about O'Brien. I went over this morning to the kitchen to get the milk for my cats and when I came back that's when they told me O'Brien was gone.'

'Jock, you spent a couple weeks with O'Brien – what did he tell you about the money and the bank job?'

'Well, sir, he told me everything about the robbery. I wish to tell you off the record and not to sign any statements because I would be in fear of my life from that dangerous man.'

'Okay, Jock – off the record so.'

'He said all the money is in Russia, and that's where is going to live when he gets bail. He had a new woman in his life. She was Russian that he met in a pub in Charlestown.'

'What else did he tell you, Jock?'

'He said that he is working for the Russian secret service and they took care of all the money. It's now in Moscow.' Detective Sweeney was gobsmacked with this information coming from Jock. 'I really appreciate you telling me all this. I will not ask you to sign it as respect your wish as you don't feel safe. Have you any idea how O'Brien was getting to Moscow?'

'He did mention that the agents were going to fly in under the radar and land a small long-distance plane on a beach and collect him. But, sir, I don't want to believe a word he told me. I let it go in one ear and out the other, and I'd advise you to do the same. O'Brien is probably at home this minute hiding under the bed from the wife.'

'That's all so, Jock. Thank you very much for talking to me, I really appreciate it.'

Fred the head left the visit worrying that he might have over done the lies.

Detective Sweeney returned to the police station and walked in to Detective Rice. 'I was up to see Jock in prison.'

'Oh, that's the guy they all call Fred the head, because he is a nut case.'

'He's not that nutty now. He is a really nice guy. He gave me a bit of very interesting information on the robbery. First of all we can kiss our fucking arses goodbye to the fucking money.'

'You mean the money is gone?'

'Yes them fucking Russian migrant workers did the job for O'Brien. Jock told me about it all. Some of them were Russian agents handling O'Brien who is an agent for them commies.'

'You're fucking joking me.'

'No, I'm not. He told Jock the whole lot. What's more, O'Brien also told Jock when he got bail that he would be gone to Moscow. So I asked him how was O'Brien going to get out of the country when he had no identification. Jock said the agents were going to land a small, long distance plane on a secluded beach and fly O'Brien out of the country directly to Moscow non-stop. It's all as plain and simple as I told you.'

'I believe now O'Brien had all the plans ready in the event he was arrested for the robbery. I also believe O'Brien was a secret Russian agent spying on our country.'

'So the Russians got the money,' said Detective Rice.

'Yep.'

'Well, the Russian economy has doubled over the Christmas,' said Detective Rice jokingly.

Sweeney wasn't impressed. When Detective Sweeney left the room Detective Rice sat thinking to himself and said in his mind, *Is it possible that someone very intelligent has set up this robbery to frame O'Brien the builders? Well, good luck to them, Detective Sweeney helped them get away with it.*

The media packed up and left Charlestown because the news of the escape story had dried up with O'Brien gone.

Billy and Mick arrived at Charlie's house. Charlie said, 'It's dark enough, let's go.' Down in the back shed they put on the military-style clothing. Billy and Mick strapped a Heckler and Koch MP5 with laser sights. Charlie strapped on his Smith and Wesson 38 six-inch barrel.

Billy and Mick were armed. This was the first time they got armed. Moving the money was the biggest risk of the job. Charlie had his night vision on. Nobody was going to take the money from them. They pushed the plane out of the shed and Charlie bolted the wings in place after extending them out. 'She is fully charged for take-off,' said Charlie. 'Now we have to go and get the money.'

Charlie took out the bigger boat so that they could all get in. He had three paddles strapped inside the boat. 'Grab the engine, Billy,' said Charlie. It was a silent outboard motor. 'So Mick, carry that battery, the boat is already wired up for this electric engine, it just makes the trip quiet and quicker coming upstream in the current.'

The three got into the boat with two large empty holdalls. They brought one torch for inside the diesel tank. Charlie put on his night vision helmet and they pushed away from the river bank. They did not use the engine going downstream in the current. The three of them paddled and the boat took up speed. They had to travel two miles. On the way down Charlie was scanning the riverbanks for poachers out at night that might see them. But if they did, they would think they were poachers as well.

'How much money are we collecting, Charlie?' asked Billy

'We are filling these two holdalls and loading them on the plane. They would be equal to two more people on that plane and that's the maximum weight I can carry.'

It only took about fifteen minutes to get downstream to the wilderness area where the money was. Charlie scanned the area before they moved on to the riverbank. There wasn't a sound to be heard in the night. They creeped from bush to bush over to where the tank was buried.

'Don't worry, lads, I did this on my own,' said Charlie, 'to get you that money.'

'We know, Charlie,' said Mick.

'Mick, you stay there by the riverbank and mind the boat. Me and Billy will go get the money.' They got to the hide out and opened the hatch and pulled out bunches of cash and stacked it in the holdalls. When they were finished the amount of cash they pulled out didn't make any noticeable difference in the tank. They zipped up the holdalls, covered up the hideout so nobody could see it and retreated back to Billy at the riverbank.

The boat was tied to a bush so the three of them got into the boat, Billy in the middle with a holdall between his legs and Mick at the front. Charlie was sitting in the back. He put the electric outboard onto the side of the board and hooked it up. He pressed the switch and the power came on. He asked Billy to untie the boat and let it off. Charlie throttled the silent engine and she slowly moved off upstream. Charlie was scanning the banks of the river with the night vision helmet. 'Nobody is around, boys.'

'That's good, Charlie,' said Mick.

The electric outboard was struggling in the current. Charlie told the boys, 'Paddle the boat for all your worth.'

The boat picked up speed with Billy and Mick paddling. Now they were going just as fast as they were coming down. 'The little outboard is a great idea,' said Mick.

'I know that,' said Charlie.

'When are you going to count the money, Charlie?'

'When I get to my destination, I will count it.' Slowly they manoeuvred the boat against the riverbank next to the plane. Charlie crept out first to scan the grounds with the night vision glasses. 'Come on, men, there's nobody around.'

Charlie changed his clothes and put on a warm ski suit. 'Its cold up there,' Charlie said.

Billy and Mick changed their clothes and put them into a bag to take away with them. They put the money in the back of the plane where the two seats were and strapped it down. Charlie had removed any extra weight inside the plane. Charlie quickly climbed into the plane and put on his night vision helmet and said, 'Here I ago, boys.'

'The best luck, Charlie,' said Billy and Mick.

Charlie started a hybrid engine on the batteries. Slowly the plane started to roll down the riverbank, all the lights on the plane Charlie had disconnected so it couldn't be seen in the dark.

Billy and Mick looked down after Charlie took up speed and the dark shadow of the plane went into the sky. 'Right, Mick,' said Billy, 'let's close up here and get out of here.'

Charlie was in the sky over the wilderness area when he turned on the petrol engine and it roared into life, he throttled it up and she started to take up speed. He had a long journey, a five-hundred-mile round trip.

Billy said to Mick as they jumped in the car, 'How long will he be in the sky?'

'I don't know,' said Mick.

'He said something about five hundred miles. Whether it's five hundred each way or five hundred both ways.'

'I don't know – he knows what he's doing anyway so he will be back before it gets bright.'

'Are we going to wait here for him to return?'

'No – we go away for a while and we come back later.'

Charlie was now at four hundred feet following a railway line with his night vision in the direction he had to go. But he also used the instruments to make sure he did not get lost. It was a wonderful starry night and Charlie was thinking to himself: *Celine couldn't imagine where I am this minute. So I better get home before it gets bright in the morning.*

The weather was fine. There was very little turbulence in the sky. Charlie was thinking to himself: *This is one flight of many I have to make. Many more to come.* Charlie was relaxed, looking at the stars as the plane made its way up the country. After an hour Charlie looked down and he could see from the terrain that he was close to the estate he was going to land in. He switched off the main engine to battery power and circled around; he could see the two-mile avenue and the mansion lit up. He lined up the plane for landing. Slowly he brought it down onto the tarmac driveway of the country estate and quickly taxied the plane up to the front door.

His trusted business friend was sitting on the steps waiting for him to land. Charlie jumped out of the plane, 'Right, I told my friends that I was going to count the money but I'm not. You're my trusted friend so you count it all. Call my cell phone before I land back at my place. Take the bags off immediately and I'll get out of here.' Charlie's friend took the bags off. Charlie finished his pee and he jumped on board the plane and raced down the driveway and lifted into the sky just as quickly as it landed.

Charlie was back in the sky and switched over to the petrol engine again. The plane was now faster because as it had less weight. It was very cold, Charlie was shivering. He had a cell phone sitting on the dashboard of the plane, just before he landed his trusted friend phoned him and said the number is, '10, 350.'

'Okay – thank you very much,' and Charlie hung up.

Charlie landed the plane back at the riverbank in silence with the battery engine. Billy and Mick were back waiting for Charlie in the shed. They quickly hurried out and help Charlie push the plane into the shed.

'How did it go for you, Charlie?' said Mick.

'It went fine, everything went like clockwork. I dropped off the money and flew back.'

'How much was in the bags?'

'There was 10,350,000.'

'Wow,' said Billy.

'My business friend will have the money transported to an office he has in Eastern Europe where we can use the cash to buy the properties in your portfolio.'

'This is the best way of transporting that money,' said Billy. 'It's a brilliant idea.'

'I know,' said Charlie, 'from A to B non-stop. When all the money is transported, I will fly you and Mick to my friend's estate to meet him.'

'Could we not just go by car?' said Mick.

'No, we will fly. It's quicker and nobody sees us.'

'How was your flight anyway?' asked Billy.

'It was good – no problems.' Charlie folded the wings on the plane. 'Help me pushed the plane into the shed and park it over there where it was and I will connect up the charger to the batteries for the flight tomorrow night.'

'Have we to go down the river again tomorrow night, Charlie?'

'We could fly it one night on and one night off, it's up to you two.'

'Flying every night, Charlie, is too much for you.'

'Okay, so you fly every other night one on, one off. So we are off tomorrow night.'

Chapter 28

Charlie paid a visit to Fred the head that morning. Fred was in his cell waiting patiently for this visit. The officer called, 'Fred Moran visit.' Fred the head jumped to his feet and went straight out to the visiting room. Charlie shook his hand and looked him in the eye with total delight. 'How are you keeping, Fred?'

'I am very good, Charlie, and how have you been?'

'Fine,' said Charlie.

'Did you tell Celine I said hello, and I will see her at the wedding?'

'I did, Fred. She said she's looking forward to meeting you.'

'What's the story, Fred?' Charlie said.

'He's gone,' Fred said.

'Okay, do you need anything, Fred? I just came to reassure you everything on my end is done. Your property is ready. When will I come back for you, because I have to make the appointment to get in the main gate with the Ivor Williams trailer and the thirty cages on it?'

'Come back for me in seven days. I will be ready so that makes it this day week Thursday morning at 10 pm.'

'Okay, Charlie, I will be ready. Have you any problems with your release?'

'My papers were waiting ten years to be signed to walk out the gate.'

'That's good.'

'Right, Fred, I will go now and remember on the day you walk out of this prison your name is Jock again. Forget about the Fred.'

'Okay, Charlie, it's Jock again. How are things at home, Charlie? Are you very busy?'

'I am, Jock.'

'I bet you are my friend.'

'I don't trust many people, Jock, but, I totally trust you, and I have a lot to tell you when I have you settled in to your new home.'

'Charlie, I will see you on Thursday, this day next week.'

'Okay, Jock, bye for now.'

*

Tonight was Charlie's fourth flight to his trusted business friend. This time he needed to collect the three million worth of diamonds he ordered from him on the last flight. The drill was the same. Charlie, Billy and Mick went down the river and got the two big holdalls full with cash and returned to the plane. They loaded on board and strapped them down and immediately Charlie went down his grass runway. In a couple of hours he was over the estate preparing to land. This time they agreed that he didn't need runway lights turned on. He told his friend that he would land in the dark with his night vision helmet. That way there was less chance of somebody seeing the plane land on the avenue tarmac.

He taxied up to the front door as usual and jumped out of the plane, and unloaded the bags. His friend Gavin said, 'Charlie, I have the diamonds you ordered. Come on in and I will show you.' Charlie went in the big double front doors. He was greeted by a magnificent marble hallway with marble pillars and marble statues which are recessed into the walls all around him.

'This is such a beautiful house, Gavin.'

'Thank you, Charlie.'

'As you know this was in the family home for over three hundred years.'

'A beautiful place to spend your life, Gavin.'

'Not bad I suppose. Anyway sit down there and have a look at the finest diamonds money can buy. Your father-in-law will be very impressed with the clarity and the flawless quality of these diamonds. Now that's a trade price of three million which could be retailed at five.'

'Thank you very much, Gavin, I really appreciate you getting me the best.'

'It's a family business, Charlie – no bother at all.'

'I better be off home, bumpy flight back again.'

'Okay, Charlie – you have a nice flight. I will move this money tomorrow morning.'

'Thank you, Gavin. You be careful, see you again the night after tomorrow night.' Charlie left the great marble hall and went out the front door, climbed on board his plane and down the runway and into the sky as silently as he landed. Gavin was looking after him and said, 'A man of many talents – soars into the sky which has no limit for that man.'

Charlie made it back in an hour and a bit, and had a perfectly smooth, silent landing on the riverbank runway with the electric engine. He taxied up to the shed where Billy and Mick were waiting for him to dismantle the wings and returned the plane to the shed to recharge the batteries again for the next flight. Billy turned to Charlie and said, 'I know you have a parachute strapped onto your front not the back.'

'Yes,' said Charlie. 'It is too uncomfortable to have it on my back.'

'The thing that bugs me Charlie is this. Are you flying high enough to bail out if you have a problem?'

'I don't know – we just have to wait and see. Let's hope there are no bailouts. I must fly under the radar. The engine on my plane is brand new, so I don't expect engine failure but also with the battery hybrid it is fail safe. Anyway that plane can land with no engines. I can glide it into any field.'

'Okay, Charlie,' said Billy, 'just worrying about you having to make all those flights on your own.'

'You remember when we were digging the Tunnel, I did say it was going to be an equal share. Well, now I ask ye. Am I entitled to more because of the extra work and risks I have to take?'

'No problem with me,' said Mick. 'You are entitled to half the money and the other half is between me and Billy.'

'That's 100% with me,' said Billy. 'You have done a lot more and put a lot more into this project.'

'I'm not a greedy man, lads, but I feel done by if I don't reward myself more for all the extra work and effort I had to do on this project. Well, anyway I must go now and meet Celine at her father's house. I got the diamonds I ordered.'

'That's good, Charlie. We will see you the night after tomorrow night for the next flight.'

'Okay, lock up the garage, I'm off.'

Chapter 29

Charlie went to Celine's father's house – the house of his dreams. Celine answered the door. 'Hello, my darling,' she said.

'Hello, darling. Did you have a nice day shopping for the wedding, darling?'

'I did and I got the nicest wedding dress you can imagine but you cannot see it. You're not allowed. It's tradition for the groom not the see the dress until the morning of the wedding.'

'I know that, darling. I don't want to see it until the morning of the wedding. It won't be long now and you will be my wife.'

'I can't wait, darling, to be your wife. And I can't wait for you to be my husband, darling.'

'I suppose I better go and speak to your father in private about the wedding. He said he was taking care of everything anyway. Well, it is time I ask for your hand in marriage.'

'He's in the study.'

'Okay, darling, give me fifteen minutes.' Charlie walked into the study and sat down with Joseph.

'Hi, Charlie.'

'Hi, Joseph. I'd like to have a chat with you about the house.'

'This house, Charlie?'

'Yes, Joseph, this house.'

'Okay, and then we talk about the wedding.'

'Okay.'

'Joseph, how much did it cost you in total to build this house and furnish it – every penny you paid?'

'This house cost me 1800,000 euro and change.'

'Right. I know your family are Jewish diamond dealers.'

'That's right, we are diamond dealers for a long time. That's where the money is, Charlie.'

'Well, I know nothing about diamonds or dealing in them. When I was working abroad last year, I saved a man's life who was about to commit suicide. It's a long story, Joseph, he was a diamond dealer. When I was finished building his mansion, he called me into the room and said. "You are a good man. Only for you I would not be here now. I have got over the dark patch in my life. I have enough money to live a hundred lives. So I have a gift here for you which I want you to take without any hesitation. I will not tell you how much they are worth but there are now yours." So he handed me this little pouch with diamonds in it and said they are yours. So, Joseph. I had them valued and the wholesale value is about three million, so they are worth above that. I will hand you this bag of diamonds which you can dispose of through your family if you give me and Celine this house as a wedding present.'

Joseph took the diamonds into his hand and poured them out onto a white sheet of paper. He took out his little eyeglass to have a look without saying one word. 'I am very impressed, these diamonds are of the highest quality and clarity I have seen in a long time. That man that gave you them really appreciated you saving his life. You know your diamonds are worth one million more than the cost of this house and more than that as well.'

'I just told you, Joseph – for the inconvenience I will give you that bag of diamonds for you to give this house as a wedding present to me and Celine.'

'I will accept your offer without hesitation. I will build the same house for half of them diamonds.'

'I don't care how much you make. I just want this beautiful ten-bedroom house for me and Celine to spend our lives in.'

'I tell you what, Charlie, I will give you the house, and I will also pay for the best wedding that money could buy as well as the house.'

'It's a deal.'

'There's only one agreement to all this.'

'What's that, Charlie?'

'Your daughter Celine must not know about this deal. The house is a wedding present, Joseph.'

'That's fine with me, Charlie.'

'So we shake on it then.' So Charlie left the room and joined Celine. They then went out for a meal and went to McCarthy's pub.

*

Later that night in McCarthy's pub Celine turned to Charlie and said, 'I am waiting all night for you to tell me what Daddy said.'

'Sorry, darling, for keeping you waiting. Daddy said I am allowed marry his daughter Celine. And also, we discussed the wedding and I explained I could only afford a small wedding. So he said he is paying for everything and it would be the best wedding money can buy. It was his daughter's day and he wouldn't have it any other way.'

'I'm so happy, darling, that Daddy said yes. We would be in some mess if he said no.'

'I know, darling, I can't imagine it. So what date have you picked, darling?'

'I have the wedding booked since the 1st January. I just reserved the hotel. Daddy told me to do it. It could be booked out.'

'So when is it, darling?'

'You are going to marry me next Sunday three weeks.'

'That's fine with me, darling. I must go and get my wedding suit. What would you like your new husband to wear?'

'Well, we are getting married in your cathedral because it's so beautiful, what you wear would make no difference to me, just be there.'

'Okay, darling, I will go shopping in a couple of days and get everything I need. I have the rings picked out. Daddy came with me for them.'

'How many people are going to be at our wedding?'

'Well, I counted about four hundred. That's including anybody I could think of on your side, but you must go through the list as soon as possible and include anybody I forgot. We have a lot to do darling before our wedding day.'

'I will leave it to you. Women are very good at making plans to get married.'

Chapter 30

Charlie got out of bed at 6 am to go to the new farm that he purchased for Fred the head. At the farm, he had a brand-new Ivor Williams trailer with thirty brand-new cages strapped to it. He hitched up the trailer to his jeep and started the long journey to the prison to pick up Fred the head and the thirty cats. It was ten am when Charlie arrived at the main gate of the prison. He had clearance and permission to enter the prison with the trailer and cages to collect Fred Moran and his cats. The prison was more than happy to cooperate and see Fred leave once and for all. Charlie drove around to the boiler house where Fred the head was waiting for him.

'Good morning, Charlie.'

'Good morning, Jock. Are you ready to go?'

'I'm up half the night collecting my cats to get them ready to go. I have some of the giddy ones in boxes. We will load them first.'

'Okay, Jock, let's start loading.' It took over an hour to load all the cats into the cages because some of them didn't want to go in. Outside the old wing block that Jock lived on for years was two big cardboard boxes with all Jock's personal belongings. Charlie looked and thought, *Thirty years in prison and this is all his worldly possessions.* Eventually they were ready to roll.

'Climb on board, Jock, we are driving away to your new freedom.' They drove out the gate and down the road a bit when Jock said, 'Pull up at the pub. We must go in there for a drink.'

'Okay, Jock we will park here right outside it.' They walked in the door and they both sat at the counter. The barman came over and immediately said, 'Hello, Jock.'

And Jock said, 'Hello, Geoffrey.'

Charlie thought he was hearing things but ignored it. Charlie turned and asked for a pint of Heineken. And the barman said to Jock, 'Is it the usual Scotch whiskey for you.'

Jock nodded, 'Yes.' Charlie looked at both the barman and Jock bewildered. *How do these two know each other*? was running through Charlie's mind. When the drinks were served the barman bent down under the counter and pulled out a bundle of letters and handed them to Jock. He said, 'Here's a few letters for you.'

Jock removed the rubber band from the letters and started opening them. Charlie was more bewildered. Jock had a quick read of each letter after removing the money from each one and sliding it into his top pocket. So they had their drink and said their goodbyes to the barman. Jock picked up his bundle of open letters and put them in his jacket pocket as they were leaving the pub. Charlie did not say a word until they were in the jeep. The barman shouted, 'Give me your new address to forward on your mail.'

'Oh yes, I forgot about,' said Jock and walked back and gave him the address on a piece of paper. Jock shouted back, 'I will call in when I'm around this way.'

'Look forward to seeing you, Jock.'

When they got into the jeep Charlie said, 'Jock what the fuck did I just witness in the pub?'

'Yes, Charlie, that is where all my letters come to.'

'But how do you collect them.'

'I will tell you laddie a lot of dark cold wet windy nights I go for a few drinks. I put on my big old coat, a big scarf and woolly hat and I leave the prison by the old disused back gate. I have a key for that gate for last ten years.'

'You're fucking joke on me. You're fucking shitting me, Jock.'

'No, I'm not.'

'Holy fucking, baloney, you fucking foxy locksy Jocksey, what the fuck. Who is sending you the money, Jock?'

'Well, you heard the story, Charlie.'

'What story?'

'Remember all those people that supposed to have gone up the fucking chimney.'

'Yes, Jock, I heard the story.'

'Well, I have news for you.'

'None of them went up the chimney. I slipped them all one by one out the back gate after I secured new identification for them which was addressed to the pub.'

'You fucking fox. And everybody thought you murdered them.'

'No Charlie–they all escaped. I slipped them out the back gate. And they were carried out of the country all arranged by me.'

'I can't fucking believe it. You have me fucking gobsmacked. I can't fucking believe it. You fooled them all.'

'So were you, Charlie. Every month they send me money to the pub so that I can buy cat food.'

'So tell me, Jock – where the fuck is O'Brien.'

'Yes, Charlie. Mr O'Brien now resides in South America. He was fed up with the wife anyway and he did have a few million stacked away. So I told him he was getting convicted of the biggest bank robbery in history and would spend the rest of his life in jail. In other words, Charlie, I frightened the seventeen types of shite out of that fucking idiot. I knew after a day or two that that fool could not organise a robbery of that calibre. I put all the little pieces of the jigsaw together very quickly. I knew I had to get rid of him as fast as I could for you. It was difficult to get the passport because of the Christmas backlog. But I got rid of him, and he really appreciated what I did for him. Also, Charlie, when O'Brien went missing there were making enquiries to what O'Brien had told me when working in the boiler house with me. I got a visit from Detective Sergeant Sweeney the lead investigator on the case. From the information about O'Brien using Russian builders on the cheap it gave me a good story to tell that fucking Sergeant Sweeney.'

'What did you tell him, Jock?'

'I told him O'Brien spilled the beans in a moment of weakness. O'Brien told me everything. He said he was a

Russian agent and that is why he had Russian builders working for him. Some of them were secret service from Russia and took care of the whole robbery. O'Brien told me that when he got bail the Russian agents were going to land a small long-distance plane on a beach and fly him out of the country for ever.'

'Did he believe it, Jock?'

'Yes, he did. Every word of it.'

'A right fucking twat that Sergeant Sweeney. You amaze me, Jock, I can't fucking believe you pulled the wool over my fucking eyes.'

'Well, Charlie, you're a clever man yourself. You had me fooled as well.'

'When did you work out that it was me that did the robbery?'

'The first day I had O'Brien in the boiler house, he was crying like a baby. I knew then that fool could not have the intelligence to rob that bank. So the process of elimination began. And I put all the two and twos together and came up with you being the richest man in the country.'

'I was going to tell you anyway, Jock.'

'I know you were. Talk about me being a foxy Loxley. You're the biggest foxy Loxley I have ever had the pleasure to meeting. I'm so glad that you picked me to help you, Charlie. Your secret is safe with me so help me, God.'

'I know that, Jock, I know that. Jock, I owe you big time for helping me.'

'How much land did you buy me, Charlie?'

'You have one hundred acres, Jock.'

'That is more than enough, Charlie.'

'You should get in a woman to help you and you'd never know what would come about. How old are you, Jock?'

'I am fifty years old. I went to prison when I was twenty.'

'Jock I'm going to send you to the Philippines to find a wife that will look after you and the cats for the rest your life. My friend Billy will go down there with you and look after you. You can't go down there on your own.'

'Yes, I look forward to going down there. Charlie them Filipino women are very beautiful.'

'Jock, you will come home married to the most beautiful woman a man could imagine.'

'Charlie, when am I going?'

'Very soon, a few weeks. I must get someone to live in the farm to look after the cats while you're away.

'Jock, is there anything else that I could do for you to show you I really appreciate what you have done for me?'

'Let me think about that for a few days, Charlie.'

'The next farm on the right-hand side, Jock, is yours.' They drove up the drive way. Charlie took out a remote control and pressed it. Two big gates started to open. 'Look at all the security fence all around that I installed for you, Jock, not even a cat will get through that.'

'It's absolutely beautiful, Charlie. Absolutely beautiful. I'm over the moon. You couldn't imagine a more beautiful piece of land. The house looks beautiful, Charlie. The sheds are ideal and the barn. Thanks, Charlie, you owe me nothing else.'

'No, Jock, I owe you a lot more. I will put a financial package in place that you will have money every month, more than you need.'

'Thank you, Charlie.'

'You won't be short, Jock. And your Filipino wife, I will get Billy to give her family fifty grand to help them after she leaves the country. That way you will have a really loyal beautiful woman.'

'What more can I say, Charlie?'

'Nothing, Jock, just enjoy yourself. Let's unhook the trailer and unload all the cats. We will carry them into the big barn in the cages. When you have the door locked you can let them all out.'

'Okay, let's get to work so, Charlie.'

When all the cages were loaded into the big barn Charlie said to Jock, 'I'm off now, I will call and see you in a few days.'

Chapter 31

Back in Charlestown, Detective Sergeant Sweeney was under severe pressure to hold onto this case. He knew in his heart that this case is over, but he had no choice but to grasp at the straws that were left. He called to see O'Brien's wife. Mrs O'Brien, 'Yes, Sergeant Sweeney. You can call me Caroline, Sergeant Sweeney.'

'Okay, Caroline.'

'What can I do for you, Sergeant?'

'It's about your husband.'

'I don't know where he is. There is no point asking me questions about him when I know nothing.'

'I just called to see how you were and see if you can throw any light on it for me. Did you know your husband had a Russian girlfriend?'

'I didn't.'

'He met her in a nightclub in Charlestown.'

'That's news to me, Detective Sweeney. So tell me she is beautiful as well and twenty something.'

'Also I know the whereabouts of your husband right now.'

'Well, tell me then.'

'Off the record you must not repeat this.'

'Okay, Detective.'

'Your husband is in Moscow. It's very unlikely that your husband would ever contact you, but he might. If he does, will you please let us know? Did you know, Mrs O'Brien, that your husband was working for spies, giving them information on this country. That is how the whole robbery came about.'

'It's all new to me, Detective. My husband told me nothing.'

'You see, Caroline, your husband was trained to keep his mouth shut no matter what. And that's what he did when we arrested him. My advice, Caroline, is to close all joint bank accounts and move any money in them to your account. He has a lot of money but bitter sweet revenge could strike from afar.'

'I will do that tomorrow, Sergeant Sweeney.'

'Goodbye, Caroline.'

'Bye, Sergeant.'

Charlie was in town preparing for the wedding. He had got all his new clothes and made all the necessary arrangements. Charlie was flying out tonight to have all the money out of the country in Eastern Europe. The flights at night time had now become routine. The tank with all the money was now down to halfway. Over one hundred million had been transferred for to launder in properties. Charlie, Billy and Mick had invested in different types of property and they were now rich men.

Charlie came up with one last idea to send the cops down the wrong road further. He picked out some large notes from the money that were brand new and went in sequence. He got his trusted business partner Gavin to transfer an envelope with these notes in it. The notes were posted from Moscow to Mrs Caroline O'Brien's addressed with a letter stating. *I'm sorry for any inconvenience I have caused you. I now have a new life here in Moscow. I am getting married again to the woman I love. I enclose a small amount of money – five hundred which I will send you from time to time. You don't deserve anything from me because you did not love me for years. You also have the money in bank accounts.*

The letter was already typed out and in the envelope. It would be posted in Moscow in a few days and arrive at Mrs O'Brien's within the next week.

Three days later, Detective Sweeney was in his office looking out the window and saying to himself, *It's time to go.*

He picked up a cardboard box of files and emptied it into the corner of the room. He went to his desk and put in his photograph frames of his wife and children. He took out all his personal letters from the drawer and put them in the box. He took out his Smith and Wesson 38 special from its holster and put it on the desk. He undid the holster straps, folded them up with the revolver back inside. He took out his police shield and put it with the gun and then put his box under his arm and headed out to the reception. He handed the gun and shield to the duty sergeant and said, 'I won't be needing them again. I'm fucking out of here.'

He walked out the front door and looked back. He said in his mind, *Them Gestapo bastards will never get the pleasure to talk down to me again.*

Chapter 32

One hour after Detective Sergeant Sweeney resigned, the chief walked into Detective Rice's office and said, 'Congratulations, Detective Rice. You are now a sergeant. It gives me pleasure to promote you here today. As you know Sweeney's history.'

'I know, Chief. It's sad for a man's career to end like this.'

'Well, he knows the score. You don't blow your chips on one hand of cards. That is exactly what he did. The investigation into the biggest bank robbery in history is now becoming history itself as unsolved.'

Detective Rice knew in his mind not to go down any more roads with this investigation because he was now Sergeant Rice and it is not good to fuck it up.

The following week Mrs O'Brien called into the police. 'Hello, Sergeant, my name is Caroline O'Brien. Could I speak to Detective Sergeant Sweeney?'

'Mrs O'Brien, I must inform you that Detective sergeant Sweeney has retired.'

'Could I speak to his colleague, Detective Rice?'

'You mean, Detective Sergeant Rice?'

'Yes, sir.'

'This way please.'

The Sergeant opened the door of Rice's office and said, 'A lady is here to see you – Caroline O'Brien.'

'Come in, Caroline.'

'How do you do, Detective Rice?'

'I'm fine. What can I do for you?'

'Well, Detective Sergeant Sweeney came to me last week and asked me to contact him if I received anything from my husband, Noel. You know, Noel O'Brien?'

'Yes, Caroline, I know.'
'Well, I received this letter this morning from Moscow.'
'That's interesting. Could I have a look at it?'
'Yes, Detective.'

'Rice opened the letter addressed to Mrs Caroline O'Brien. In it he found five brand new notes, one hundred euro each. The serial numbers of the new notes were in sequence. Rice immediately suspected that they were from the bank robbery. He said to Mrs O'Brien, 'Let me check the serial number list.'

Detective Sergeant Rice turned to Caroline and said, 'They are not on the list of notes from the bank. Did you get any letter with it?'

She did get a letter but she said, 'No, Detective, I didn't.'

'Well, somebody sent you some money and they are not on the list of stolen money so they are yours. Just go and spend it.'

Mrs O'Brien left the office and walked down the street and she said to herself: *Why are you protecting my rat bag husband. What about if his fingerprints were on the note and that would prove in court my husband robbed the bank. I could not live with myself it I was the rat that put my husband in prison for ever.* Caroline took out the note and tore it up with the envelope and put it into a wastepaper bin.

Detective Sergeant Rice was looking out the window saying to himself: *Sweeney was fucking right, he is in Moscow, and those notes are on the list, but I'm not taking any more skeletons out of the closet on that investigation and end up just like Sergeant Sweeney did so as far as I'm concerned, this investigation is over.*

*

It was two o'clock in the afternoon. Charlie, Celine and all the guests were in the cathedral. This was the biggest wedding to take place in this county in the last fifty years. Celine's father Joseph put on the most expensive show you could imagine. The wedding was like the Oscar's awards night.

The priest said to Charlie, 'You may now exchange vows with Celine.'

'I, Charles Anthony Green, take Celine Dayoni from this day forward to be my lawful wedded wife for richer or poorer, for better for worse, for in sickness or in health until death do us part. So, help me, God.'

'Celine you may now exchange your vows.'

'I, Celine Dayoni, take Charles Anthony Green from this day forward to be my lawful wedded husband for richer or poorer, for better for worse, in sickness or in health until death do us part. So help me, God.'

'I now pronounce this couple to be husband and wife from this day forward. You may kiss the bride.'

The End